THE UNTOUCHABLES

Robert Stack as Eliot Ness in classic pose.

THE UNTOUCHABLES

TISE VAHIMAGI

bfi Publishing

First published in 1998 by the
British Film Institute
21 Stephen St, London W1P 2LN

The British Film Institute is the UK national agency with responsibility for encouraging
the arts of film and television and conserving them in the national interest.

Cover design: Swerlybird Art & Design
Cover images: Robert Stack as Eliot Ness in *The Untouchables* (Paramount Television)
All illustrations from BFI Stills, Posters and Designs

Set in Minion by Fakenham Photosetting Limited, Fakenham, Norfolk
Printed in Great Britain by St Edmundsbury Press, Bury St Edmunds

British Library Cataloguing-in-Publication Data
A catalogue record for this book is available from the British Library
ISBN 0–85170–563–4

Contents

Acknowledgments

Thanks are due to Paul Taylor and Bryony Dixon, who read and commented on parts of the manuscript; Ed Buscombe, Rob White and Andrew Lockett, who were sympathetic editors; Cherry-Ann Chandler and Sean Delaney of the (then) BFI Library and Information Services, who were extremely helpful and cooperative in my various areas of research; Bruce Ricker (New York), who very kindly put out a dragnet for the original two-part *Desilu* episode; Tony Mechele, David Meeker and Markku Salmi, all of whom listened patiently and offered ideas and suggestions during the early stages of the work. Thanks are also due to Paramount Television, distributors of *The Untouchables* series.

Introduction

From October 1959 to September 1963, America's ABC TV network broadcast one of television's most original series, *The Untouchables* – Desilu Productions' semi-documentary stories of Treasury agent Eliot Ness and his small squad of Prohibition agents' fight against the gangster elements of the late 1920s Chicago underworld. The series ran for a total of 118 hour-long episodes over a five-year period.

The Untouchables was perhaps the most violent series in television history. It presented four seasons of furious action and frequently over-the-top gangster characterisations, all for the most part set against the bloody backdrop of Al Capone's corrupt Chicago.

When TV network executives called for 'action' they meant 'violence', which is exactly what *The Untouchables* gave them. And the viewers hungrily lapped up the weekly instalments of blazing machine-gun battles, shoot-outs with bootleggers and gangsters being taken 'for a ride'. It elevated the then third-rated network to top position, for the first time in ABC TV's history.

Due to its relentless violence, as well as the obvious references to Latin types as prominent gangsters, the series brought controversy to Desilu and the ABC network, culminating in the uncomfortable publicity of a congressional investigation. In their defence, *The Untouchables* producers claimed that its stories were based on historical fact: the series' source book, Ness's 1957 autobiography, and the actual Prohibition-era characters and events, all of which depicted violent times. How else could that brutal era be truthfully and realistically shown? The fact that the real Eliot Ness never actually fired a weapon during his Prohibition investigations and never even came close to any of the gangsters and killers seen in the show was casually overlooked. But it didn't matter.

However, Desilu's flair for overextending dramatic licence brought them a barrage of complaints from various directions, including the FBI, the Capone estate, the US Prisons Bureau and, perhaps the most powerful of them all, the Italian-American anti-defamation groups. The latter's argument, that the series tarnished all Americans of Italian extraction as gangsters, was correct inasmuch as Italian gangsters of 1920s Chicago accounted for only 25 per cent of the corruption that ruled that city. The national publicity accorded Al Capone at the time (self-promoted mostly) overshadowed all other ethnic criminal groups, the largest of which, incidentally, were Irish.

Eventually, Desilu gave in to the tidal wave of demands and diluted the fourth (and final) series down to incorporate vague WASP types as gangsters and 'motivated' scenes of violence. Unfortunately, the viewers became less than motivated. The ratings slumped, and the series faded into TV history.

Of contemporary significance was the fact that *The Untouchables* represented a sudden burst of comic-book-style action in a television period when such 'drama' was still regarded as being supposedly believable. That *The Untouchables* sparked, flashed and then faded in the years leading up to the events in Dallas in late 1963 perhaps reflected the television climate of the time more accurately than any socio-political study of the early part of that decade. In a common-sense approach, *Untouchables* director Walter Grauman observed: 'The show is dramatic fiction with documentary authenticity.'

In its attempt to create an entertaining reflection of dramatic history, *The Untouchables* was not only exploitational, it was colourfully theatrical. But then, the only way to show that particular period in history was, perhaps, to caricature it, something that the contemporary TV watch groups failed to observe. The elements of extreme violence were undoubtedly an accurate reflection, as was the Italian element of corruption. But by going completely overboard in its small-screen translation, the series attracted an enormous viewer following (the ratings), while at the same time courting controversy: a peculiar history lesson represented in comic-book style. Appropriately, the series' historical foundation was questioned and probed. Although it certainly didn't set out to be any kind of a pseudo-educational programme, its 're-enactments' of history as a part of 'popular' programming soon whipped up a tornado of controversy simply because the show *was* popular. In essence, *The Untouchables* was simply a guys-gats-gals form of television escapism. It never pretended to be anything else.

For good, bad or otherwise, the series and its own production development remains one of the most exciting periods of US television history. While it spanned various visual and dramatic styles, from film noir (the mood and setting) to the Western (the face-to-face shoot-outs), *The Untouchables* also attracted an impressive line-up of guest performers. Hollywood veterans, such as Claire Trevor, J. Carrol Naish, Lloyd Nolan, William Bendix, Thomas Mitchell and Richard Conte, shared the screaming-tyres and barking-shotguns action with such stars-to-be as James Caan, Robert Duvall, Peter Falk, Jack Klugman and Robert Redford. Recurring guest players Bruce Gordon and Nehemiah Persoff brought colour to their respective roles of Frank 'The Enforcer' Nitti and Jake 'Greasy Thumb' Guzik. All shot under the careful eye of seasoned directors such as Stuart Rosenberg, Paul Wendkos, Robert Florey, Tay Garnett, Ida Lupino and Laslo Benedek.

The Untouchables was a televisual alarm clock that awoke both the almost sedate viewing nation and the rather complacent US television industry.

PART ONE

(l. to r.) Abel Fernandez, Nick Georgiade, Robert Stack, Paul Picerni.

1 'Seven Against the Wall' (1950–58)

Sometime around ten-thirty on the morning of 14 February 1929 in a garage at 2122 North Clark Street, Chicago, Illinois, there was a disturbance. Seven men – six belonging to the North Side George 'Bugs' Moran gang and one simply a civilian hanger-on – were shot to death against a wall by four of Al Capone's mob, two of whom were dressed as policemen. The cold-blooded event was to become known as the 'St Valentine's Day Massacre'.

This mass gangland assassination, when reported by the national press, outraged the American public. At the same time it became the firing-pin that projected the newly elected President Herbert Hoover and the US Treasury's Special Intelligence Unit finally to put an end to the underworld empire of 'Scarface' Al Capone, a murderous industry of bootlegging and gambling, narcotics and prostitution estimated to be worth some $100 million.

A 26-year-old Prohibition agent named Eliot Ness, along with a special squad of Prohibition enforcers the newspapers were to tag 'The Untouchables', was then given licence to start his own war of attrition against the Capone outfit. It was to be the beginning of the end of the Capone era of organised crime in Chicago.

*

From points of history to historical points of television. The American television police drama (in contrast to the TV detective/private-eye drama series) has been the most popular programming genre, with the exception of the situation comedy, since the mass television boom of the early 1950s. Many of the earliest US crime series were actually popular radio shows that had been transferred to television: for example, *Dick Tracy* (ABC, 1950–51) and *Mr District Attorney* (ABC, 1951–52).

In retrospect, the two great turning points of US television crime/police drama came with, initially, the daily televising of the Senate Crime Investigation Committee's New York hearings in March 1951 and, then, the following year's première of Jack Webb's long-running *Dragnet* series.

The live transmissions of the US Senate's inquiry into organised crime, led by Senator Estes W. Kefauver, swept the country (the inquiry included the testimony of such underworld figures as racketeer Anthony 'Tough Tony' Anastasia, former Bugsy Siegel girlfriend Virginia Hill and Mafia boss Frank Costello; the hearings, incidentally, popularised the term for refusing to answer questions, 'on the grounds that it may incriminate me' – the US Constitution's Fifth Amendment).

The Kefauver hearings became the nation's number one TV programme: '*Variety* and every other trade publication have characterized those telecasts as a new and irresistible form of public entertainment' (*Films in Review*, May 1951). The television fascination with real-life crime and criminals was under way.

Although a series called *Crime Syndicated* (CBS, 1951–53), featuring dramatisations of cases from the files of the Senate crime probe, appeared some four months before *Dragnet* (NBC, 1952–59), it was the latter show that actually introduced the 'based on police files' standard for crime/police series to come, as well as the semi-documentary style of narration. *Gangbusters* (NBC, 1952), *Highway Patrol* (syndicated, 1955–59) and *Official Detective* (syndicated, 1957) continued this successful trend of basing their stories on actual police cases.

These popular series and others during the 1950s fed the viewer a steady diet of semi-documentary law and order while 'a little like voyeurs, the audience gets to ride in the back seat of the squad car and experience firsthand the seamy side of life'.[1]

By the late 1950s the interest in case-history crime/police drama had attracted the attention of feature-film-makers. There were several reasons for this. Most notable among them included the real-life 1957 barbershop assassination of notorious Murder Inc. overlord Albert Anastasia (brother of 'Tough Tony'); the November 1957 police discovery of a top-ranking Mafia summit meeting convened in the little village of Apalachin in New York State (where some sixty-two Italian-American mobsters had gathered); and, perhaps, also because the 1950s saw the end (due to natural causes) of many of the Prohibition-era gangsters who had survived the internecine gangland warfare of the period – such as George 'Bugs' Moran, former Capone aide Jake 'Greasy Thumb' Guzik and Capone mentor Johnny Torrio. Collectively, it was these events that first appeared to attract film-makers to exploit the criminal careers of the country-boy (and girl) killers of 1930s rural America.

Don Siegel's *Baby Face Nelson* (UA, 1957) was the first of this batch. Released in November, it starred Mickey Rooney in the title role as the 1934 Public Enemy Number One. The *Variety* review noted that 'in the interest of historical accuracy, the cast wears depression days styles and the footage is replete with chase scenes involving Model A Fords and dated "touring" cars' (*Variety*, 6 November 1957). The *Variety* reviewer's prediction that the film 'might even start a new gangster film cycle' was to prove more accurate than they had perhaps realised.

The big-screen success of *Baby Face Nelson* was quickly followed up by *The Bonnie Parker Story* (AA, 1958), about the infamous early 1930s gunwoman, which was paired with the same unit's *Machine Gun Kelly* (AA, 1958), featuring Charles Bronson as the undersized sadist. At the first opportunity, this capitalisation on infamous 1930s outlaws saw producers rushing to register rights to, among others, the (relatively short) life story of 'Pretty Boy' Floyd and the violent saga of the rum-running and kidnapping activities of Detroit's The Purple Gang.

The increasing popularity, and to a certain extent the glorification, of these twentieth-century outlaws, albeit in exploitation B-movie form, led the film companies into excavating filmable histories of the urban gangster: Al Capone of Chicago, Dutch Schultz and Legs Diamond of New York, to name but three. Also, perhaps, a certain inspiration came from the 1957 publication of a loosely autobiographical work, co-written by UPI sports writer Oscar Fraley and a former

Brooklyn-born Italian-American Alphonse Capone, called 'Scarface Al'.

Prohibition agent called Eliot Ness, *The Untouchables* (New York: Julian Messner, 1957).

The book, detailing Ness's battles against the Chicago underworld, was written after Fraley had spent a night drinking with Ness. 'He started telling me all his Al Capone stories,' Fraley said in a 1987 interview. 'I said, "Why don't you write a book?" He said, "You write it." ' Ness devoted more than two years to working on the book. But, unfortunately, on 16 May 1957, shortly after approving the final galleys, Eliot Ness died suddenly of a heart attack.

Although the book went on to serve as the basis for the TV series and later the 1987 film with Kevin Costner, the real Eliot Ness never saw the remarkable success of the television series he had helped create. Fraley went on to write two sequels to *The Untouchables* – *The Last of the Untouchables* and *Four against the Mob*.

While Ness and Fraley's book depicted the Prohibition era of Chicago (1929–33), with Ness as 'a handsome six-footer whose hand-picked gangbusters destroyed the myth of Capone's immunity', the actual history of Ness, Capone and 1920s Chicago is a little less 'gangbuster' and rather more procedural, though most of the unpalatable violence and corruption was still there.

Brooklyn-born Italian-American Alphonse Capone (called 'Scarface Al', a sobriquet that arose from a scar received in a barroom fight) had been summoned from New York to Chicago in 1919 by Chicago crime boss Johnny Torrio. Capone's ruthless efficiency, especially when dealing with gangland rivals, elevated him to a position as Chicago's leading Italian gangster by 1925. With the imposition of Prohibition on 16 January 1920, Capone had been among the first to recognise the new (Volstead) Act's money-making possibilities, most notably that of bootlegging. By 1927 Capone's bootlegging operations were bringing in around $60 million. Eventually, in 1929, President Hoover ordered the Treasury to convict and imprison Capone for good (previously, through corruption, he had always managed to evade 'serious' jail terms). The Justice Department's Bureau of Investigation (the early FBI), under its director J. Edgar Hoover, refused to take on the seemingly impossible task. The Prohibition Bureau was too inept or corrupt. It was left to the Treasury's Special Intelligence Unit to pursue the job in an effort to convict Capone for, of all things, not paying his taxes.

Toward the end of 1929, Eliot Ness suggested to his Chicago superior, Alexander Jamie (who was also Ness's brother-in-law), that a special squad of men – mainly single and with no Chicago connections (and therefore regarded as least likely to succumb to bribery or threat) – be recruited to investigate and raid Capone's breweries, as well as conduct wiretap surveillance on the bootlegging operations. Given the official go-ahead, Ness and his special team (of ten men) began their campaign of harassment of Capone's illicit breweries, stills and speakeasies.

Apparently immune to bribery in a racket-infested city, the squad was described by one front-page story in the following way: 'Eliot Ness and his young agents have proved to Al Capone that they are untouchable.' A caption writer adopted it for another newspaper and over a picture of the squad printed the words: 'The Untouchables'. The wire service picked up the phrase and so were born 'The Untouchables'.

*

While TV Westerns and contemporary private-eye series largely dominated the television schedules of the late 1950s, two single productions appeared that presented stories dealing with real-life urban gangsters of the past: 'Albert Anastasia: His Life and Death' (CBS, 27/2/58), for the anthology series *Climax*, and 'Seven Against the Wall' (CBS, 11/12/58), for *Playhouse 90*. Having just hit the headlines some months before, the grisly story of *Climax*'s 'Albert Anastasia' unfolded in Eva Wolas's production which, after an opening scene in which Anastasia (played by Eli Wallach) is gunned down in a barber's chair, traced his sordid life from a young punk on the waterfront to his role as lord high executioner of Murder Inc., the underworld execution squad. The story, told in flashback, culminated with a reprise of the opening-shot assassination. The *Variety* reviewer approached the chilling story with some caution: '[Wolas] may have been open to blame, to be shared by director Buzz Kulik, in permitting actual shooting to be shown twice. ... Actual gunning down of a victim is rarely shown. The shot may be fired but the victim not shown at point blank' (*Variety*, 3 March 1958).

If this was unsettling to contemporary viewers and critics, then the *Playhouse 90* presentation at the close of the year must have truly alarmed the TV audience and the viewing professionals. It was a signal of what was to come. 'Seven Against the Wall', with Franklin Schaffner directing Howard Browne and David Davidson's ninety-minute teleplay for producer John Houseman, was a careful chronicle of the mechanics of Al Capone and his mob as they plotted the murder of Bugs Moran, Capone's chief competitor in Chicago-land crime. The meticulous plan backfired and seven men were slaughtered while the main target, Moran, was somewhere else. 'Within the natural limitations of its documentary form, [the production] was something exceptional,' commented *Variety* (15 December 1959). 'As live television, it was a notable achievement.' A large cast, with over forty speaking parts, performed the grim spectacle of the build-up to the 1929 St Valentine's Day outrage in a flawless re-creation of the period; the principal players included Paul Lambert as Capone and Dennis Patrick as Moran.

Historically and chronologically, in terms of the TV crime drama genre, 'Seven Against the Wall' was an appropriate production with which to end 1958, for in the early part of the following year *Desilu Playhouse* would present the conclusion to the Al Capone story and at the same time usher in a new and sophisticated excursion into the past with their explosive two-part episode, 'The Untouchables'.

2 'The Scarface Mob' (1959)

It was Roger Corman's *I, Mobster* (20th-Fox, 1958), released in January 1959, that started off the new year with the revival of the gangster genre. The Corman production, generally regarded as a 'well-turned-out melodrama' dealing with the rise and fall of a fictitious gangster, was soon overshadowed by the first of the two major gangster film productions of 1959 (both concerning Al Capone) that would impress and influence film-makers and television producers to launch the third great gangster movie cycle since the popular *Little Caesar/Public Enemy/Scarface* wave of the early 1930s.

The March release of *Al Capone* (AA, 1959) was an immediate hit with both the critics and the audiences. 'A tough, ruthless and generally unsentimental account of the most notorious gangster of the prohibition-repeal era,' hailed *Variety* (11 February 1959). 'Allied Artists' *Al Capone* is a contender for top boxoffice.' And that it certainly proved to be.

Inspired by *Climax*'s presentation of 'Albert Anastasia' the previous year, producers John Burrows and Leonard Ackerman had hired 'Anastasia' scriptwriters Malvin Wald and Henry F. Greenberg to come up with something similar about the life of Al Capone for Allied Artists. Back in 1949, incidentally, Wald had worked on producer Robert Rossen's *The Undercover Man* (Columbia, 1949), the story of a Treasury agent who is sent to Chicago to get evidence against Capone for income tax evasion. The American censors of the time, however, refused to allow the producers to mention Al Capone by name and they were forced to refer to him obliquely as 'The Big Fellow'. A similar problem now plagued the production of *Al Capone*, as Wald recalled:

> We had no sooner started our research than J. Edgar Hoover, in the course of a speech opposing the making of movies about gangsters, named our picture as one of those he thought should not be made. His attack on gangster films had been set off by a movie which had been a sensational glorification of the notorious killer known as Baby Face Nelson.[2]

The first draft screenplay of *Al Capone* was turned down by the Hollywood censors and the story had to be rewritten from the viewpoint of an honest police officer who had witnessed the rise of the Capone organisation, but was powerless to fight it in the face of political corruption and public apathy. When the film finally made it to the screen (with Rod Steiger in the title role; Ernest Borgnine had been the original choice), the action-packed story of Capone's violent rise to criminal power was an instant success, prompting the largest number of release prints ever ordered by Allied Artists for one of its productions: the initial order of 500 prints was increased to 600 for domestic distribution.

Al Capone (AA, 1959): (l. to r.) Al Ruscio, Rod Steiger and Louis Quinn.

In retelling the infamous story, *Al Capone* contrived no happy moral. As *Variety* (11 February 1959) reported: 'Using a semidocumentary style, with occasional narration from an honest cop, James Gregory, it is made clear that this story of a generation ago has particular pertinency today.' *The Untouchables* would later echo this position, as Larry James Gianakos observes: 'Look no further than *The Untouchables* for an exegesis on the unsteady balance of Good and Evil. Ness triumphs only in the physical sense, but the cesspool triumphs spiritually.'[3]

It may also be interesting to note, from the production side, that James Gregory's Sergeant Schaeffer was modelled on the real-life Chicago detective Captain John Stege, who had also been one of the original St Valentine's Day

Massacre investigators. Gregory would later appear as another real-life 1920s policeman, New York detective Barney Ruditsky, in *The Lawless Years* series.

Leading up to the release of *Al Capone*, writers Wald and Greenberg were delighted with television's concurrent interest in Prohibition-era gangster themes. After the December 1958 presentation of *Playhouse 90*'s 'Seven Against the Wall', Wald and Greenberg commented that 'This serves as a 90-minute trailer for *Al Capone*. Several millions of the younger generation, who'd probably never heard of Capone, now know what and who he was, certainly making our picture a more potent box office draw' (*The Hollywood Reporter*, 5 February 1959). They also expressed their pleasure that (by that time) Desilu had plans for *The Untouchables*: 'Our picture, which embraces all of Capone's nefarious career, will probably still be playing when Desilu's story hits the TV screens.'

On the TV production side, two 1920s-period series just about managed to beat Desilu and *The Untouchables* to the post, albeit unintentionally.

The first, *Pete Kelly's Blues* (NBC, 1959), with producer-director Jack Webb's adaptation of his own 1955 Warner Bros feature, premièred on 4 April 1959 for what would be a very short (thirteen-episode) run. Set largely in a 1927 Kansas City speakeasy, the Webb series revolved around a Dixieland bandleader (played by William Reynolds; by Webb in the film) who somehow managed to get himself involved in various non-musical adventures connected with underworld types. Occasionally, he and his Original Big Seven Band would belt out a couple of rousing Dixieland standards of the period (Dick Cathcart's trumpet standing in for Reynolds's solo spots; Matty Matlock on clarinet leading the offscreen sidemen), but the emphasis on the lead character was that of a combination gumshoe and Dixieland trumpeter. The series, despite its Roaring Twenties background, was more in keeping with the then popular TV private-eye genre of the late 1950s than the Prohibition-era gangster drama with which it appeared to identify itself.

Much closer to the gangster era, and genre, was producer Jack Chertok's hoodlum-ridden series *The Lawless Years* (NBC, 1959–61), featuring James Gregory as police detective Barney Ruditsky. (Chertok, incidentally, had been a producer on the one-and-two-reelers of the *Crime Does Not Pay* series (1935–47) for MGM during the 1930s.) Originally titled *Ruditsky* when it started production in January 1959, the series was based on the memoirs of the one-time first-grade detective who headed up the New York Police Department's Gangster Squad and who was a persistent nuisance to such 1920s New York crime kingpins as bootleggers Waxey Gordon, Dutch Schultz and Lucky Luciano.

The series, however, had a peculiar start-stop-start history. It premièred on 16 April 1959, just four days ahead of Desilu's 'The Untouchables', and ran until September; it then it presented a second season that ran from October to December 1959. Although *The Lawless Years* was something of a forerunner to *The Untouchables*, the series ceased production at the end of 1959. It was not until the overwhelming success of *The Untouchables* series during its first (1959–60) and second (1960–61) seasons that the producers put the show back into production for one more season, starting in May 1961.

For the most part, *The Lawless Years* presented stories about real 1920s gangsters but used fictitious names; however, certain notorious types were directly featured in several episodes: for example, 'The Dutch Schultz Story', 'The Al Brown

Story' (the capper of this one being that 'Al Brown' was an actual pseudonym for Al Capone, who had fled New York for Chicago), 'The Jack "Legs" Diamond Story' and the two-part 'The "Mad Dog" Coll Story'.

At the start of the series, the *Variety* review was undecided: 'This isn't the usual cops 'n' robbers type of show; the accent and viewpoint lean on the criminal rather than the cop' (*Variety*, 21 April 1959). But midway through the first season, and following 'The Untouchables' two-part triumph, the opinions had formed:

> Another look at *Lawless Years* immediately conjures up comparisons. Since the first viewing shows have come along such as 'The Untouchables' and Capone orgies of crime.... [The] main trouble with Jack Chertok's production is that it's as dated as the stories it tells. Techniques have changed since Ruditsky wore a NY police badge. (*Variety*, 15 July 1959)

The Lawless Years would not be the last TV programme, or even feature film for that matter, to be judged against the production standards and story pace of Desilu's 'The Untouchables', which would deliver a certain atmosphere and energy, and project a powerful influence over all gangster-themed productions to follow in the immediate years.

*

The story of the Desilu production company began during the shooting of the 1940 RKO musical *Too Many Girls*, when Lucille Ball, the film's lead, met Cuban-born bandleader Desi Arnaz, also in the cast. Married in November 1940, the couple then purchased a ranch in Chatsworth, California, which they christened Desilu. In July 1948, Ball began starring in *My Favorite Husband*, a radio series for CBS about a scatter-brained housewife and her banker husband. After the show's second year, she was approached by the network about converting it into a TV series. The sponsor, cigarette manufacturer Philip Morris, expected the series to be produced live from New York, standard network procedure at the time. But, preferring to reside in Los Angeles, Arnaz proposed that they shoot the series on film; this meant that the series would be shot before a live studio audience in LA, the film prints being hurriedly despatched over to the East coast for later transmission. Also, the expense of such an unusual production process meant that Ball and Arnaz would have to take a salary cut. The deal was struck, and the pair formed Desilu Productions, with Arnaz as president and Ball as vice-president, to produce the show.

I Love Lucy, as it was now called, débuted in October 1951, and set the standards for sitcom production that still prevail. The highly popular series continued to run on CBS throughout the 1956–57 season, during which time Desilu Productions, building on the equipment and facilities it had amassed to produce *I Love Lucy*, developed into a high-profile Hollywood television factory, producing or providing services on the sitcoms *Our Miss Brooks* and *Make Room for Daddy*, and the dramas *The Lineup*, *The Whirlybirds* and *The Walter Winchell File*, among others.

In September 1957, Desilu purchased the RKO Gower and RKO Culver studio facilities from General Tire, bringing its total holdings to thirty-five sound-stages and a 40-acre backlot. Just over a year later, in December 1958, the company went public. During the 1958–59 season, Ball continued her *Lucy* series as a monthly

13

show, 'The Lucille Ball–Desi Arnaz Show', as a part of the hour-long anthology *Westinghouse Desilu Playhouse*, under the sponsorship of Westinghouse Electric. The *Desilu Playhouse* series, which ran on CBS from 1958 to 1960, would also produce and present the two-part episode 'The Untouchables' in April 1959.

In March 1960, Arnaz and Ball were divorced. Their financial empire, including their holdings in Desilu, was split evenly. Arnaz continued to head Desilu Productions, but in November 1962 he sold his portion to Ball, who assumed his post as president. She eventually sold the studio in 1967 to Gulf & Western, which turned it into Paramount Television.

*

In 1958, Desilu announced their purchase of the Fraley–Ness book, following the dissolution of an option held by producer Ray Stark. 'Desi had read the book and asked me to read it,' recalled Desilu executive Martin Leeds:

> I suggested that we buy the motion picture and television rights. Little did I know that his plan was for him to do a feature picture with *him* playing the part of Eliot Ness. I asked him, 'Des, do you really believe that the world is waiting for Ricky Ricardo [Arnaz's role in *I Love Lucy*] to pull the plug on Al Capone?' He said, 'Okay, not such a good idea, sport. Put it in the library and let's wait for an opportunity to do it.'[4]

Arnaz's purchase of *The Untouchables* came as quite a surprise to many in the industry in view of his firm stance against violence-laden television productions: 'Our policy has been never to do shows of violence of a psychopathic nature, of adultery, or such things.'[5] Nevertheless, in late January 1959, it was announced that *The Untouchables* would be screened as *Desilu Playhouse*'s first two-part episode. Writer Paul Monash was brought in to do the script adaptation and, by mid-March, Quinn Martin had been assigned as producer and Phil Karlson (his first TV work) appointed as director. The per-hour production cost was set at a record $300,000.

Quinn Martin, following service in the Army Air Corps during the Second World War, had returned to his film-editing job at MGM (after an earlier apprenticeship). He soon began writing scripts, then became a writer and producer at Desilu, where he went on to produce 'The Untouchables' two-parter. In 1960, after leaving Desilu, Martin formed QM Productions and went on to turn out such popular series as *The Fugitive* (ABC, 1963-67), *12 O'Clock High* (ABC, 1964–67), *The FBI* (ABC, 1965–74), and *The Invaders* (ABC, 1967–68). His company later produced *The Streets of San Francisco* (ABC, 1972–77), *The Manhunter* (CBS, 1974–75) and *Most Wanted* (ABC, 1976–77).

For the lead role of Eliot Ness, Desilu approached film actor Van Heflin, who quickly turned it down because of approaching film commitments and an unwillingness to be caught up in the daily grind of working on a weekly TV series. A 'name' movie star was required, since the show's high costs meant that it had to be sold in Europe as a feature film after its US television première, as Robert Stack later recalled:

> Originally, it was to be a feature picture. We shot it in four weeks as a feature. It was for European release. It was filmed in wide screen.... It was to be cut into two one-hour film shows on *Desilu Playhouse*. Desilu got $125,000 for each show. That made

$250,000. But the picture cost $500,000. The other $250,000, plus maybe a million or two profit, was to be made up from theatre showings. (*TV Guide*, 5 December 1959)

With Arnaz's first choice of Van Heflin not now available, Desilu offered the part to Van Johnson, who accepted and was signed up. But just a few days before shooting began on the first of the two hour-long films, Van Johnson pulled out; Johnson, apparently, had thought he was to receive $10,000 *per* episode, but Desilu had actually set the actor's rate at $10,000 for the whole production. With just a weekend to find a replacement for Johnson, Arnaz and the Desilu producers held a series of frantic long-distance telephone conferences. Robert Stack was suggested and Arnaz managed to track him down on the Sunday and offer him the Ness part. Stack, who had only just finished working on the period swashbuckler feature *John Paul Jones* (WB, 1959), initially refused, eager to pursue his career in feature films. However, persuaded by the forceful advice of his agent William Shiffrin, he soon changed his mind. 'For the two hours you'll get ten thousand dollars,' Arnaz had told him. 'And if it goes to a series, seventy-five hundred per episode, plus fifteen per cent of the profits, which I will give you in Desilu stock.'[6] In addition, Stack also sold a dummy corporation, Langford Productions (taken from his father's name, James Langford Stack), to Desilu, which in effect made him a partner in the production. (Earlier names rumoured to play Ness, incidentally, had been Alan Ladd, James Arness and Fred MacMurray.)

By the week beginning 16 March, shooting was under way at Desilu-Culver, and on Tuesday 17 March *The Hollywood Reporter* announced that Stack had taken over the Ness role from Van Johnson. The principal cast included Keenan Wynn, Neville Brand, Barbara Nichols, Patricia Crowley, Bruce Gordon, Joe Mantell, Paul Picerni and Bill Williams. Cinematographer Charles Straumer and film editor Robert L. Swanson were also brought on board. Transmission of the two-part drama was set for 20 and 27 April.

*

Since 1957, famed radio and newspaper columnist Walter Winchell had been supplying stories and narration (based mainly on his own experiences) for the crime anthology series *The Walter Winchell File* (ABC, 1957–58) for Desilu. Despite some internal troubles at Desilu with the crusty old Winchell, the reviews of his show had been good, but the *Winchell File* was slumping in the ratings. The series went off the air in March 1958 (but was later revived in syndication). On 2 April 1959 it was announced that Winchell had been signed up as narrator for 'The Untouchables'. According to Desilu producer Bert Granet:

> Desi Arnaz felt an obligation to Walter after the demise of *The Walter Winchell File* and asked him to narrate a pilot of a new one-hour series. Executives at ABC [for which the series would be made], Walter later claimed, had blackballed him from the assignment, but Arnaz and producer Quinn Martin insisted. According to Arnaz, 'Walter gave the show a feeling of truth and immediacy. His machine gun delivery was very, very important to the show. Without Walter it wouldn't have been the same.'[7]

*

On the eve of the screening of 'The Untouchables' (part one), Stack commented

15

The original *Desilu Playhouse* 'Untouchables' squad line-up.

cautiously: 'You've got to be awfully careful. If you go into a series, you run the risks of overexposure, of being typed, and then there's the matter of personal pride' (*The Hollywood Reporter*, 20 April 1959). He need not have worried, for events in the wake of 'The Untouchables' success would relieve Stack of his actorly 'pride' and caution.

At this point a brief outline of 'The Untouchables', part one, would be helpful:

> While Al Capone is serving a short term in prison in Philadelphia (a ten-month sentence for carrying a gun), his bootleg empire continues to thrive under the leadership of his aides Frank 'The Enforcer' Nitti (Bruce Gordon) and Jake 'Greasy Thumb' Guzik (Bern Hoffman). On learning that the police are being bribed on a large scale, Eliot Ness (Stack) receives permission from US District Attorney Beecher Asbury (Frank Wilcox) to recruit a squad of seven hand-picked men, headed by Joe Fuselli (Keenan Wynn), a reformed gunman. They discover the location of secret breweries by tapping telephone wires and, using a special armoured truck fitted with a battering ram, demolish them.

Following the presentation of part one of 'The Untouchables' (*Westinghouse Desilu Playhouse*/CBS, 20/4/59; 9–10 p.m.), the major trade paper reviews were split. *The Hollywood Reporter* (22 April 1959) followed its usual industry-accommodating line:

> Though there was plentiful action and suspense in this first half ... direction that the plotting took indicated that next week's finale will be even more power-packed. There's little gainsaying that those who caught the first half won't want to miss the second.

In contrast, the *Variety* review for the same day was, at first, less than enthusiastic:

There is little distinction in the present series. The Capone yarn comes off just as any other film on this subject. There is no dissertation on the conditions that permitted a Capone to crop up, except through the background narration by Walter Winchell, who gives this opus a little more depth than it deserves.

But then the TV ratings came cascading in. The opening hour swamped all opposition in the time slot. It scored a 31.8 Trendex rating (a TV ratings system based on telephone calls) in its first half of transmission and a 29 in its second. The programme averaged a 30.4 rating and a whopping 56.3 audience share for the hour.

No sooner had the first part been screened than Desilu Productions announced plans for a theatrical release of 'The Untouchables'. 'Following final cutting for TV of the second one-hour episode,' reported *Variety* (22 April 1959), 'producer Quinn Martin will despatch a crew to Chicago to film additional footage for the feature version.' 'The Untouchables' was budgeted at $300,000 per one-hour episode; with additional shooting, editing, scoring and processing, the theatrical version would go as high as $1 million.

Part two, screened the following Monday (27/4/59), concluded the Ness–Capone story:

> Released from jail in March 1930, Capone (Neville Brand) reorganises his outfit and has Ness's fiancée, Betty Anderson (Patricia Crowley), assaulted in her home. He breaks the wire tap, kills a Ness informer and hires Jimmy Napoli (Frank De Kova) to murder Ness. Ness escapes death when Fuselli is mistaken for him and machine-gunned. Soon afterward, the government puts together a case which leads to Capone's conviction on charges of tax evasion, and he is sentenced to eleven years in prison.

Part two drew the following enthusiastic trade responses: 'Where last week's episode sublimated actor prowess for plot development,' said *The Hollywood Reporter* (29 April 1959), 'the windup not only offered more suspense and crackling action, but characterizations shone through with devastating clarity. . . . It's difficult to point out highlights when hardly a minute passed without something worthy of comment.' *Variety* (28 April 1959), for a change, agreed: 'Phil Karlson's direction kept the long two-hour show [reviewed complete] fast-paced and accurate. Camera work was striking. Desilu pulled out all the stops for producer Quinn Martin on this one, striving for authenticity and production scope.'

Now, despite his initial caution in taking on a TV role, Stack was flushed with success: 'I've received more reaction in one week on my role in "The Untouchables" than on anything I've ever done in features, including *High and the Mighty*.'

The programme's second part managed to beat even its own previous week's Trendex rating by seven points with an average 37.5 and an enormous 64.8 audience share.

Director Phil Karlson, to his surprise, was immediately flooded with offers of work on the strength of the *Desilu Playhouse* production. At the same time, Desi Arnaz was also trying to rope him into an exclusive deal with Desilu. It was, apparently, due to Karlson's earlier feature-film work, with such film noir dramas as *Kansas City Confidential* (UA, 1952), *99 River Street* (UA, 1953) and *The Phenix City Story* (AA, 1955), that the Desilu producers had assigned him 'The Untouchables'. Karlson later received an Emmy nomination (for Outstanding

Keenan Wynn (left) as former gunman Joe Fuselli and Robert Stack as Ness in the two-part 'The Untouchables'.

Directorial Achievement in Drama) for 'The Untouchables'. The 1960 Emmy Awards (for the period March 1959 to March 1960) also honoured Charles Straumer, for Outstanding Achievement in Cinematography for Television, and Ralph Berger and Frank Smith, for Outstanding Achievement in Art Direction and Scenic Design, for their work on the programme.

Following Allied Artists' instant box-office blockbuster hit with *Al Capone* earlier in the year, and *Desilu Playhouse*'s 'The Untouchables' achieving the highest Trendex ratings of the year, the race by Hollywood film-makers to hop aboard the new commercial bandwagon had really begun. The MPAA Title Bureau saw the rush for registrations for *Murder Inc.* by 20th Century-Fox; *Legs Diamond* and *Lucky Luciano* by the independent Transnational; *Elmer (Trigger) Burke* and *Brink's Robbery* by Columbia; *Guns, Girls and Gangsters* by United Artists; and *Organized Crime, Story of Bugsy Siegel, Dutch Schultz, Mobster, Louis Lepke* and *Mafia, USA* by Warner Bros (the latter studio, by chance, were already sitting pretty with the Mervyn LeRoy production, *The FBI Story*, which was ready for release). At the same time, Desilu was approached by three major distributors seeking US release rights to 'The Untouchables' feature version, something Desilu hadn't anticipated until the Trendex score for part two came in. There was some irony in the fact that Allied Artists had brought in *Al Capone* for $550,500, whereas Desilu had spent close to $600,000 on its two-hour telefilm.

The Scarface Mob, as the re-edited theatrical version was entitled, was released in the UK by Warner-Pathé in early 1960, and, eventually, in the US by the Desilu Film Distributing Company in October 1962. The film's running times were, variously, at 97 and 98 minutes for the UK and European release; 105 minutes for the US release. It was released in France as *Tueur de Chicago*.

Then, in early May 1959, Desilu made a surprise announcement that they had sold 'The Untouchables' as a series to the ABC TV network (at a cost of $110,000 per episode). The purchase created bad feeling between Desilu and CBS TV, on whose network *Desilu Playhouse* had originally appeared. CBS TV's contention was that it was unfair for the production company to sell off a programme to a

Neville Brand's Al Capone on his return to Chicago in the *Desilu Playhouse* two-parter.

19

Robert Stack's Ness hacking into Capone's beer vats.

rival network which had been nurtured and presented by CBS. 'Everyone thought the show would be a one-shot affair,' recalled Stack in his autobiography:

Once we caught Capone, there wasn't supposed to be anywhere else to go. No one realized at the time that we were formulating a branch of theatre wherein the character actor (a different one each week) became the star.

Tom Moore [programming head] of ABC was the first to envision a series based on the two-parter. At that time, Bill Orr, an executive of Warner Brothers, was trying to sell a show called *Public Enemy* using all the great stock footage from the Edward G. Robinson–James Cagney era. Orr was told to forget it. 'No one is interested in downbeat stories about gangsters during prohibition,' said the executives. That same week, 'The Untouchables' hit the air and broke the Nielsens [a ratings system based on 'audimeters' inserted in a sampling of television sets] wide open with a 36.1 rating.[8]

With Quinn Martin now appointed as executive producer for the weekly ABC TV series, the contract with the network called for them to finance a minimum of twenty-six one-hour episodes. In essence, ABC and Desilu would each own 35 per cent of the show, and Stack's Langford Productions would hold 25 per cent. Shortly after, Stack announced that he would star in only eleven of the first twenty-six episodes, but would host and narrate all of them. He stipulated that he wouldn't otherwise touch a weekly series that would make him unavailable for feature film work and other outside commitments. His non-exclusive deal with Desilu allowed him to take off for Japan in mid-May to start work on Andrew Stone's *The Last Voyage* for MGM.

In late May, Quinn Martin contracted Norman Retchin and Charles Russell as alternating producers for the new series, which would begin shooting in mid-July after Stack had completed location work in Japan. Retchin and Russell would each produce three episodes back-to-back on a revolving basis. Simultaneously, Harry Fried was appointed as story editor for the series. It was later announced, on 26 June, that Desilu were in negotiations with Nelson Riddle, as series composer (Wilbur Hatch had supplied the music for the original *Desilu Playhouse* production).

However, the real fireworks were still to come. *The Untouchables*, as a series, was set to première in October 1959.

3 'The Untouchables': Season One (1959–60)

Although the 'The Untouchables' two-parter had been such a rousing success, due largely to the determined direction of its storyline, the question of where to lead the series now posed a problem. An hour-long TV series about Eliot Ness, starting where the Fraley–Ness book began, suddenly seemed impossible. Ness's leading federal agent, Fuselli, had been killed and Capone sentenced in the *Desilu Playhouse* original. In effect, the Ness–Capone story had been told; so, to avoid an uncomfortable flashback, the series would begin where the two-parter had ended. Ness and his squad would now chase, for the most part, gangsters other than Capone's Chicago outfit.

Shooting on the first episode of the new series, 'The Empty Chair', began on 10 August 1959. Nehemiah Persoff was signed up by executive producer Quinn Martin to guest-star as Capone syndicate bookkeeper Jake 'Greasy Thumb' Guzik. Simultaneously, Jerry Paris was signed up for the role of Agent Martin Flaherty, joining Robert Stack, Nick Georgiade as Agent Enrico Rossi and Abel Fernandez as Agent William Youngfellow.

By now, Nelson Riddle was also under contract to write the original theme music, which he later recorded for Capitol Records (LP: *The Untouchables*, Capitol T/ST-1430, 1960; it was later nominated for the Composer's Award at the 1960 Grammy Awards). By reputation the top arranger in Hollywood during the 1950s, Nelson Riddle had worked with many of the best singers in the business, including Judy Garland, Ella Fitzgerald and Dinah Shore. Much in demand for his rich orchestrations and thick instrumentation, his orchestra provided music for many television shows. Perhaps his most TV famous composition, outside of *The Untouchables*, was 'Theme From Route 66' in 1962.

Period authenticity was to be maintained throughout the series: clothes, cars, dialogue, weapons – all had to be in keeping with the 1920s setting. Also, in order to give the show a semi-documentary quality, actual newsreel footage was inserted where possible to enhance the period atmosphere. Since no one was sure how long the series would last, all the period cars and trucks had to be rented. With the demise of *Pete Kelly's Blues*, Jack Webb had found himself stuck with fifteen vintage cars dating back to the early 1920s. Although Webb wanted to sell them outright, Desilu Studios' transportation head Aaron Dorn offered to rent the vehicles, which included such classic items as a 1933 Pierce Arrow, a 1932 Buick taxicab, a 1932 Packard, a 1928 Dodge, a 1932 Model A Ford and a 1932 Buick police car.

Then, in late September 1959, alternating producer Norman Retchin left the production having completed only two episodes. He was replaced by former

Behind Closed Doors (NBC, 1958–59) producer Sidney Marshall; this short-lived spy drama, incidentally, had starred Bruce Gordon as a counter-espionage chief.

While Mervyn LeRoy's law and order saga, *The FBI Story* (WB, 1959), a glossy propaganda film for the Federal Bureau, opened in October to 'good box-office prospect' reviews, the television highlight of the new season was the first episode of *The Untouchables* on Thursday 15 October 1959.

'The Empty Chair', from a teleplay by David Karp (with story by Ernest Kinoy), took up the story from where the *Desilu Playhouse* presentation had ended. Over the closing scene from the *Playhouse* original (as Capone is led out of the Chicago courthouse after sentencing), Winchell's Gatling-gun narration introduced the new tone and setting:

> Chicago, May 5th, 1932. After seven months of legal delays, Al Capone, the most notorious product of the nation's experiment with Prohibition, was on his way to federal prison. To serve eleven years for income tax evasion. On hand, to watch the mobster leave, was Eliot Ness, chief of the unique federal squad known as The Untouchables. The special unit that had worked for eighteen months to bring Al Capone to justice. For these men, the end of the Capone career was just the beginning of an era of violence. The king of the hoodlums had left a vacant throne behind him. The next man to claim it would pay for the privilege in bullets and bloodshed.

Following Capone's imprisonment, there remained six logical successors to his syndicate chair. One of them, Frank Nitti (Bruce Gordon), cut the figure to four by machine-gunning two of the 'cabinet' in a barbershop. Only the cunning wisdom of Jake Guzik (Nehemiah Persoff) keeps Nitti from taking the leadership by force, as he persuades his rival that they should go into legitimate businesses as a front for their illegal activities.

'As a two-parter last season, "The Untouchables" scored with enough impact to precipitate its development into a continuing series,' observed *The Hollywood Reporter* (19 October 1959). It continued:

> In its debut hour as a weekly presentation, this expansion seems to be justified. Production remains big, direction and scripting are carefully geared to action without aborting the documentary fact premises and, if shockingly gory at times, at least the producers can claim a reporting-on-history privilege that could conceivably do some good in arousing the public to the evils of syndicated crime.

The *Daily Variety* review for the same day was equally enthusiastic:

> John Peyser's direction of this crisply-penned teleplay ... stirs all the script's spicy ingredients into a brisk, suspenseful finished product that keeps the viewer alert throughout. It is a precise, inventive piece of directing, aided by Charles Straumer's energetic camera work, general production efficiency, and the efforts of a good cast obviously stimulated by, and up to, the creative demands of those guiding and coordinating the overall attack on these chronicles of law and crime.

The Untouchables appeared to be off to an encouraging start.

However, by episode two, 'Ma Barker and Her Boys' (22/10/59), Desilu and *The Untouchables* were in trouble. Jeremy Ross's teleplay saw Ness and his team pursue the middle-aged bank robber Ma Barker (Claire Trevor) and two of her sons

Abel Fernandez and Robert Stack anticipate some action.

to a small Florida resort where, after a vicious gun and grenade battle, they are killed by Ness and the police. The FBI, whose case it originally was in 1935, complained to Desilu at this gross misrepresentation of the historical facts, if not the actual credit. The following statement had to be added, and was later heard over the end credits: 'Desilu Productions wishes to point out that the FBI, although not being featured in tonight's programme, had the principal jurisdictional responsibility of the Barker case, and was responsible for the handling and eventual solution of it.'

'The Jake Lingle Killing' (5/11/59) returned Ness to his proper place and time in Chicago, although once again the real Ness had nothing to do with the actual

Jake Lingle case. The teleplay, by Robert C. Dennis and Saul Levitt (from the latter's story), used the June 1930 slaying of corrupt *Chicago Tribune* reporter Lingle, who had apparently fallen out with Capone, as the background for a fictitious plot about Ness's alliance with a private detective in a move against a bootlegging outfit. Although the episode opens with a reconstruction of the Lingle killing (he was shot dead by a single assassin in the subway station of the Illinois Central Railroad on 9 June 1930), the story departs from the facts from that point. Jack Lord and Charles McGraw co-starred, with Herb Vigran as the overconfident Jake Lingle.

The ABC network and *The Untouchables* continued to dominate their 9.30–10.30 p.m. slot for their third consecutive showing on Thursday 29 October 1959, and racked up Trendex ratings of 24.5 and 26.3 for the half-hours, leaving NBC in second position with 18.6 for *The Tennessee Ernie Ford Show* (NBC, 1956–61) and 18.6 for Groucho Marx's *You Bet Your Life* (NBC, 1950–61) quiz show. At the bottom of the ladder was CBS's *Playhouse 90* presentation of George Bernard Shaw's 'Misalliance', which started at 12.9 and fell to 9.7 during its second half.

Meanwhile, Desilu had signed Joseph Shaftel to produce five episodes for broadcast from mid-December. Also, Robert Stack had now renegotiated his contract to appear in many more than the eleven episodes he had originally asked for.

*

The target of the St Valentine's Day Massacre became the subject of 'The George "Bugs" Moran Story' (15/11/59), written by David Karp and directed by Joe Parker. Lloyd Nolan guest-starred as Moran, playing him as a gentleman gangster who was careful not to harm the small son of the president of a growing trucking union, kidnapped in order to muscle his way into taking control.

The real George Moran, in fact, was a slow thinker given to periodic rages so abrupt and unmanageable that newspapers called him 'Bugs'. He had assumed leadership of Chicago's North Side Gang following Capone's assassination of the previous boss, Dion O'Banion, in November 1924. By 1929 he was Capone's main rival and strongest opponent in Chicago. But, still, bootlegging business was after all business, and Moran received a major portion of his carriage-trade booze supply through Capone: Old Log Cabin whiskey smuggled in by Detroit's Purple Gang. Aware that the price he paid Capone left him with little profit, Moran found another supplier of a cheaper brand, but his customers soon rejected it and demanded the return of Old Log Cabin. He went back to Capone but, in a clever strategy, Capone cut him off. Moran's idiot solution was to hijack Capone's Detroit supply, which led to the bloody event of 14 February 1929. With his gang now wiped out, Moran turned to paper crimes and was eventually arrested in connection with counterfeit and forged traveller's cheques. After languishing some twenty years in prison (Ohio State Penitentiary and Leavenworth), he died of lung cancer on 25 February 1957.

With few 'name' Chicago gangsters to hound, Ness and *The Untouchables* went in pursuit of East coast gangsters early on in the first season. 'The Vincent "Mad Dog" Coll Story' (19/11/59) was the first of these fictitious excursions to New York. Charles Marion's teleplay had Ness track Coll (Clu Gulager) to Churchill Downs on Kentucky Derby day. Coll had kidnapped the favourite horse to spite

Dutch Schultz (Lawrence Dobkin, who would play the role again for *The Untouchables*), who had bet $100,000 on the steed. Ness, incidentally, was also after Schultz for income tax evasion in this episode. Eventually, Coll returns the horse but attempts to shoot him down with a high-powered rifle during the Derby. Ness shoots Coll down instead.

While the episode's plot came strictly from the imagination of the scriptwriter, Clu Gulager's striking performance of the New York psychopath was spot on. The orphaned son of Irish immigrants, the real Vincent Coll grew up in New York's 'Hells' Kitchen'. Hated by police and criminals alike, he developed a particular fixation with the destruction of bootlegger Dutch Schultz, and was, perhaps, the most sadistic killer of his time. He was twenty-three when he died, machine-gunned to death by his own gang in a Manhattan telephone booth on 8 February 1932.

Following this, Ness and his squad travelled to yet another territory in pursuit of Walter Leganza, a ruthless hijacker and kidnapper, in the 'Tri-State Gang' (10/12/59) episode. William Bendix gave a suitably brutish performance as Leganza, the leader of the gang which had terrorised Virginia, Maryland and Pennsylvania from 1933 to 1935. The actual 1930s gang hijacked trucks, chaining drivers to trees (depicted in a particularly brutal scene in the episode in which Bendix coldly machine-guns a helpless driver); murdered a messenger in a $60,000 payroll robbery; and kidnapped a Philadelphia bootlegger named Willie Weiss for $100,000 ransom, eventually settling for $8,000, but then killing Weiss anyway.

At the climax of the episode, Leganza is captured by Ness when he fractures both legs falling into the bear pit at a zoo, where Ness had him cornered. The real Leganza did in fact break both his legs after a 30-foot leap while eluding police (and not Ness), but still got away, only to be arrested later in his hospital bed and executed in the electric chair at Richmond, Virginia, in 1935, for the murder of the payroll messenger.

alias Dutch Schultz, was the subject of 'The Dutch Schultz Story' (17/12/59), from a teleplay by Jerome Ross and Robert C. Dennis (and story by Ross). *The Untouchables*' version of the story saw Ness and his squad get Schultz on a tax case (a charge originally made by Thomas Dewey, then the chief assistant US attorney for the southern district of New York State). Lawrence Dobkin again played Schultz, as an appropriately dark and menacing figure; a role Dobkin would return to one more time in the second-season entry 'Jack "Legs" Diamond'.

In 1935, when the actual Schultz was on the run from Dewey's income tax conviction, he foolishly bragged to his underworld associates his intention to murder Dewey. Since the killing of the attorney would have drawn too much 'heat' on them, they decided to eliminate Schultz before he could kill Dewey. In a Newark restaurant, in October 1935, Dutch Schultz was gunned down with three of his gang, apparently on the orders of New York crime boss Charles 'Lucky' Luciano.

*

While the notorious 1930s extortioner and murderer Louis 'Lepke' Buchalter (his nickname meant 'butcher' in Yiddish) was never featured as a central character in an *Untouchables* episode, he was represented in two third-season stories: 'Hammerlock' (21/12/61), where he was played by Robert Carricart, and 'The Maggie Storm Story' (29/3/62), in which the role was taken by Joseph Ruskin. That Buchalter was never presented as a Ness antagonist in the series was proabably because Desilu had exhausted the subject in an earlier special *Desilu Playhouse* presentation, 'Lepke' (20/11/59). Also, perhaps, the television Ness character might impinge on too many real-life people directly connected with the actual case, such as J. Edgar Hoover, Thomas Dewey, and Walter Winchell himself, to get away with the fictional licence. There was also the more obvious fact that the dramatic conclusion to Buchalter's infamous career took place in 1939 New York, as depicted in the *Playhouse* production.

The August 1939 surrender of the only big-time Prohibition mobster to end up in the electric chair was produced and directed by Jerry Thorpe, from a script by Adrian Spies, and starred Joseph Wiseman as Lepke, supported by Lloyd Bridges and Sam Jaffe. Walter Winchell narrated and re-created the role he had played as contact between the head of Murder Inc. and the FBI. As the *Daily Variety* (23 November 1959) reviewer noted:

> The story took up where Lepke ... 'contracted' for the gunning of those who gave him a bad time. [It was Lepke, incidentally, who had despatched the hit team that killed Dutch Schultz in 1935.] But it really didn't start moving until Walter Winchell was brought into the bargaining between 'Lep' and J. Edgar Hoover and accepted as the go-between in Lepke's surrender on a double cross. He had been promised a federal rap rather than a state fry in the chair, or so he was led to believe.

The end of this real-life story sounds more like a climactic plot-line from a 1930s Warner Bros gangster melodrama than a portrayal of actual events. Tried and convicted for a 1932 murder, Buchalter was electrocuted in Sing Sing (the New York State prison at Ossining on the Hudson River) on 4 March 1944.

*

By December 1959, *The Untouchables* began to experience cast changes. As we have seen, the series' format originally called for Stack to star in eleven out of twenty-six episodes, after which Jerry Paris would take over for the remaining fifteen episodes, using guest stars. With Stack's recent (October) decision to appear in every episode, Paris's role necessarily became a supporting one, which prompted his request to be released from his contract. *Variety* (16 December 1959) reported on the events:

> First show Desilu tried to do without him ['The George "Bugs" Moran Story'], or without the Eliot Ness character he plays, Stack said, it became immediately apparent that his absence wouldn't work. 'We realized that Ness is the focal point of the series, and if we left him out, the show just wouldn't hold together properly.' At that point he extended his contract to appear in all 26 episodes, and if options are carried to 32 segments, will appear in those as well.

It seemed like a very wise move by Stack, considering that his popularity as Eliot Ness had raised his feature-film asking price by about $30,000, to over $120,000 per picture; this alongside his Langford Productions' 25 per cent share of the show.

No sooner had Jerry Paris obtained his release from the series than Anthony George was signed up to step in as Agent Cam Allison. Stack would later demand that George get co-star billing with him.

*

By the close of 1959, *The Untouchables* was in trouble again. A damage suit for $1 million was filed in the Chicago Superior Court against Desilu Productions, CBS and Westinghouse Electric by Mafalda Maritote, sister of the late Al Capone and administratrix of the Capone estate. The action alleged that Capone's name, likeness and personality had been used for profit by the defendants in their original production of 'The Untouchables' without the consent of the Capone family.

They lost.

Attorney Harold R. Gordon, representing the Capone heirs (which also included his widow, Mary Coughlin 'Mae' Capone, and son, 'Sonny' Capone, both resident in Florida at the time), had already filed suit against Allied Artists and the exhibitors who had played *Al Capone* earlier in the year. According to Gordon, they were seeking $5 million from the film company, based on an estimated worldwide gross of $10 million. Allied Artists, however, had insured itself against just such an eventuality.

A similar situation had erupted in July 1959 when local Chicago citizen John G. Moran, son of the late George 'Bugs' Moran, had applied for a Cook County Superior Court injunction to black out a repeat screening of the *Playhouse 90* 'Seven Against the Wall' drama on a local CBS TV station, on the grounds that the play's re-creation of the St Valentine's Day Massacre caused him severe mental anguish.

The injunction was denied.

*

January 1960 witnessed a burst of gangster movie releases, stemming from frenzied production activity in the wake of the April 1959 two-parter and the subsequent series launch in October. First to hit the screens was producer Lindsley Parsons's *The Purple Gang* (AA, 1960), starring Barry Sullivan as a relentless detective and a youthful Robert Blake as the teenage gang leader who grew up to head the Prohibition-era outfit. 'It's too melodramatic to be a "semi-documentary", too episodic to be drama, and too superficial to be the deadly serious slice-of-life sermon on crime it purports to be, but it's a shocker,' observed *Variety* (13 January 1960). It was Parsons, incidentally, who was first appointed to produce *Al Capone* for Allied Artists, but under pressure of work he had turned the property over to John H. Burrows and Leonard J. Ackerman.

Pretty Boy Floyd (Continental, 1960), directed and written by Herbert J. Leder, was a low-budget biography of the early 1930s public enemy, starring John Ericson in the title role. But perhaps the best of this early 1960 feature crime crop was Budd Boetticher's *The Rise and Fall of Legs Diamond* (WB, 1960). Featuring Ray Danton as the seemingly indestructible Legs, the

> screenwriter Joseph Landon pictures Diamond as a psychopath, and perhaps in this way audiences will keep the character in his proper perspective. The script is constructed

28

cleverly, and Landon's dialogue is brisk and sharp. Budd Boetticher's direction could well have tipped the scales further in favour of the story's grimmer side, but in all it is good both in the light and hard tones. (*Variety*, 27 January 1960)

*

For a period of over three months, from October 1959 to January 1960, a real organised-crime event held up broadcast of three gangster-themed TV productions. The reason for this goes back to the infamous Mafia convention in Apalachin in 1957.

In November 1957, New York State police sergeant Edgar Crosswell and another trooper, having spotted a known gangland member, the son of an old gangster, followed him to the father's home just outside the village of Apalachin in New York State. There, he and his fellow officers discovered a major meeting of sixty-two of America's leading members of the Mafia, headed by Vito Genovese, 'Il Capo di Tutti Capi' ('boss of bosses') and the most powerful mafioso in New York. Historically, it brought about the official recognition of the Mafia, as well as of the Mafia in America.

During the spring of 1959, reports of that meeting were splashed across America's newspaper following the subsequent seizure of twenty-one big-time hoodlums across the country by the FBI. All were charged with conspiracy to obstruct justice and defraud the US in an indictment returned in mid-May by a Federal Grand Jury in New York.

On 21 May 1959, Desilu announced its plans for 'Meeting at Apalachin', to be shown as *Desilu Playhouse*'s opening episode for the new 1959–60 season beginning in October. But before the new season had even started, *The Untouchables*' network, ABC, was asked by the US attorney's office in New York not to broadcast their planned third episode, 'The Noise of Death', until after the trial (due to begin on 2 December) of the gangland leaders who had been arrested at Apalachin. The government felt that to show a story about an ageing Mafia leader might conceivably influence the jury. ABC and Desilu agreed to the postponement, even though it meant a difficult rush job to get a substitute episode filmed.

For similar reasons, the Department of Justice also asked for 'Meeting at Apalachin' to be held back until after the trial, fearing defence attorneys would cite the show and claim a mistrial on the grounds that the story might be construed as prejudicial.

Also, in late October, as *The Hollywood Reporter* (3 November 1959) reported, 'NBC, upon the written request of J. Edgar Hoover, has indefinitely postponed the telecast of "Crime Inc."' This production, a segment of the anthology *Ford Startime* (NBC, 1959–60), was originally entitled 'Mafia', but was changed to 'Crime Inc.' at the government's request.

The Untouchables' 'The Noise of Death' (14/1/60) was the first of the postponed TV trio to appear, and featured guest star J. Carrol Naish as an old subordinate gang boss who is forced to relinquish his power to a younger rival. Unable to resign himself to obscurity, however, he makes a final effort to assert his authority. It gets him killed. In Ben Maddow's superb script, as we follow Naish on the way to his doom, Winchell's stern narration intones:

And the time had come. Always after dinner. With good friends, good wine, and good

29

company. When a stranger would come up behind him, and hear like all the guns in the world shot off together. A terrible short noise of death.

During one of the final scenes, as the old Mafia man lies fatally wounded in hospital, his wife praying at his bedside, the following scene takes place:

NESS: 'Can he talk?'
WIFE: 'No. Nothing.'
NESS: 'He's lived this long. He's going to recover.'
WIFE: 'No. He's finished. All that blood he lost. They can't put it back. Not his blood. He was a bull. And it's hard to die. Poor man. I love him worse today than the day I married him. You know what I'm gonna do when he's gone? I'm gonna go out in the street and commit a mortal sin. So that I can go down to Hell and marry him there all over again.'

The *Daily Variety* review (18 January 1960) acknowledged the quality of the episode and Naish's performance:

Naish comes through beautifully, creating a rounded portrait of the self-made Italian immigrant who's a likeable and interesting man warranting respect despite his dirty trade and record. It's this that makes this 'Untouchables' segment different and outstanding, an escape from the ordinary black-and-white characterizations that are customary in the cops 'n' robbers shows.

The second of the postponed programmes, *Ford Startime*'s 'Crime Inc.' (19/1/60), was a less-than-gripping exposé of the way organised crime had taken to operating behind the cover of seemingly legitimate business enterprises. Directed by Delbert Mann in a quasi-documentary fashion, from Luther Davis's teleplay, 'the programme drew upon a number of tabloid stories from around the country and, cleverly enough, strung the vignettes together as though they were actual newsreel excerpts spliced together and edited' (*Variety*, 27 January 1960).

The last of the three to be screened, *Desilu Playhouse*'s 'Meeting at Apalachin' (22/1/60), had perhaps the most reason to be of concern to the US attorney, as it dealt directly with the events leading up to and including the infamous crime conclave. But even then, and possibly because the actual purpose of the meeting was still known only to the participants, the hour-long show focused instead on a minor side issue and developed it from the viewpoint of an aspiring gangster on 'trial' by the Mafia for having botched a job. On a particular point that would later reflect upon *The Untouchables*, the *Variety* (27 January 1960) review carefully observed that: 'There was some merit in the way it handled the touchy, but valid, situation of the Apalachin participants being mainly of Italian extraction. It was underscored that the guys on the side of the law also were of Italian extraction.'

Adrian Spies's teleplay concerned itself primarily with the efforts of a Chicago detective, played by Jack Warden, to expose just one of the underworld bosses (Luther Adler) who were later rounded up in Apalachin: 'Adler, in particular, gave an incisive portrayal that perfectly fit the script's description of his character ("He can talk quietly, but inside he's screamin' for blood")' (*Daily Variety*, 25 January 1960). Cara Williams and Cameron Mitchell were among the prominent supporting players. Joseph M. Newman directed Bert Granet's tense production.

*

In early February 1960, Arnold Orsatti, a club owner and moving spirit in the Sons of Italy (an ethnic Italian-American community organisation), started a ball of controversy rolling that would gain momentum and finally impact in a furore of action on *The Untouchables* in the spring of 1961. Orsatti sent out some 20,000 letters to fellow members and to Italian-American Community Relations councils throughout the state of Philadelphia urging Italian-Americans to boycott sponsors of *The Untouchables*. The TV series had evoked the protest because of its stress on the 'Mafia' and its concentration on Latin types as gangsters. The boycott list ranged from cigarettes and watches to detergents, patent medicines, toilet and kitchen articles.

*

On 25 February and 3 March 1960, *The Untouchables* presented its first two-part story (the second, if you wish to count the *Desilu Playhouse* presentation), 'The Unhired Assassin'. The story related an attempt by members of imprisoned Al Capone's mob to take over the 1933 Chicago World's Fair by eliminating crusading Mayor Anton Cermak. Though the events might have differed slightly in the two episodes, the real-life results were the same.

When Chicago Mayor William 'Big Bill' Thompson, a Capone pawn, lost to Democrat Anton J. Cermak in 1931, by the largest margin then recorded in a Chicago mayoral election, 'Cermak brought to municipal corruption a creative intelligence that fashioned a machine for the decades.'[9] With Capone's conviction, Mayor Cermak moved to recapture control of gambling and vice. This, of course, made him very unpopular with the remaining Capone mob. Something had to be done.

The script had Frank Nitti (Bruce Gordon) despatch a hit team to Miami, where Cermak (played by Robert Middleton) was vacationing to tie in with an address to be given by President-elect Franklin D. Roosevelt. Their orders were to assassinate the intrusive Cermak, and return Chicago to the outfit. A parallel plot related how a social misfit, one Giuseppe Zangara (a suitably twitchy performance by Joe Mantell), also built himself up to an assassination – that of the Democrat Roosevelt. Part one followed the Nitti death squad machinery as they moved into place, while part two brought the story to a climax, as Ness and his agents gun down Nitti's men before they have a chance to carry out the assassination; Zangara, however, manages to fire off at his target before he is overwhelmed by police. Robert Stack recalled the episode:

> We had actual shots of the assassination of Mayor Anton Cermak, when he was killed instead of Franklin Delano Roosevelt. We cut out the sequences of newsreel film and matched the newsreel footage. We couldn't improve the quality of the newsreel footage, so we worked to give our own film a grainy quality.[10]

However, while historians maintain that it was Zangara's intention to assassinate Roosevelt all along,

> revisionists claim that when, on February 15, Italian-born Giuseppe Zangara tried to assassinate President-elect Roosevelt in Miami, he was sent by Nitti and was aiming for Mayor Cermak – also in Miami on vacation. Zangara fired five shots. None hit

Roosevelt, but one did get Cermak. Though not a mortal wound, it induced peritonitis. Three weeks later Cermak died, and two weeks after that Florida executed Zangara, who had pleaded guilty. . . . He said he was aiming at Roosevelt. Nitti, who had studied under a master, would have planned better and chosen a more reliable instrument.[11]

'The Unhired Assassin' was directed by Howard W. Koch from William Spier's teleplay, and supporting players included Robert Gist, Frank De Kova (as an actual Nitti gunman, Louis Campagna), Lee Van Cleef, Claude Akins and Richard Deacon. The episodes were later re-edited into a 90-minute telefeature entitled *The Guns of Zangara*.

The following week's episode, 'The White Slavers' (10/3/60), is worth a chronological note here for being, perhaps, the first season's most uncomfortable and ugliest episode. Leonard Kantor's teleplay related how Ness sealed off the border when racketeer operations shift to Mexico, and how, with the co-operation of a re-formed ally of the operation, he staged a raid to end the activities of the mob.

Betty Field, Mike Kellin and Dick York starred in the story, in which, as Larry James Gianakos observes:

> evil runs rampant and we are actually relieved when the teleplay has concluded. One scene alone has the mob sweeping up innocent young women south of the Mexican border to be sold into prostitution, only to be tipped that Ness is on their trail and so getting rid of the evidence, literally, by machine-gunning to death the whole of their hapless victims. More than a decade after its initial showing, the dénouement still disturbs.[12]

'The Frank Nitti Story' (23/4/60) brought *The Untouchables* first season to a close with a two-in-one chapter: the background to one story was based on actual events, while the other one concerning Nitti was almost a flight of fantasy.

The Lee Blair Scott–Harry Essex teleplay, directed by Howard W. Koch, focused for the most part on how the Chicago mobsters muscled in on the movie business, with the accent on their 'protection' racket, which they called Business Engineers Inc. Ness moved in to start breaking up the extortion operations, which had begun with a number of Chicago exhibitors and snowballed into the fictitious national 'Star Theatre Circuit'.

The actual racket, at its height in the mid-1930s, was run by Hollywood-based mob men George E. Browne and Willie Bioff, and was spotlighted by industry trade papers *Daily Variety*, the Hollywood subsidiary, and parent (weekly) *Variety*, in articles written by the late Arthur Ungar (played by Frank Albertson as 'Jason MacIntyre' in the episode) when he was editor of the Hollywood paper. While the real Browne and Bioff chicanery infiltrated the IATSE (International Alliance of Theatrical Stage Employees and Moving Picture Operators), their biggest threat was exerted through the projectionists: pulling them out could have automatically darkened some 5,000–8,000 of the 19,000 theatres. Both Browne and Bioff were eventually convicted and jailed for extortion, along with others whose ties reached back to Capone's Chicago.

The other part of 'The Frank Nitti Story' was sheer teleplay invention. Ness stalks Nitti to the point where Nitti, cornered in a subway train station, resorts to a shoot-out with Ness and dies under the wheels of an oncoming train. The actual events surrounding the demise of Frank Nitti were less spectacular:

Bruce Gordon as Frank 'The Enforcer' Nitti.

When chance exposed a Hollywood extortion scheme of the outfit's, and it became clear that Nitti would be going back to jail, he could not face that prospect nor the likely decline of his power. On March 19, 1943 . . . Nitti took a stroll along the Illinois Central tracks near his Riverside home and put a bullet in his brain.[13]

*

Approaching the end of its first season, *The Untouchables* saw the departure of another one of the five rotating producers, Paul Harrison, who left to concentrate on a Western series he was creating and would produce for Paramount TV, *The*

Wrangler (NBC, 1960). In mid-March 1960, Jerry Thorpe was named by Desi Arnaz as executive producer of *The Untouchables* for the 1960–61 season. Thorpe, a staff producer-director on *Desilu Playhouse* for two years, was originally brought to Desilu in 1955 to direct the *I Love Lucy* half-hours, and had since directed many other studio-owned shows. His new post would fill the vacancy left by Quinn Martin, who was to leave in May to go into business for himself.

Late March 1960 saw the departure of co-star Anthony George, after thirteen episodes. He had asked for and received his release from his contract with Desilu so that he could be free to accept other offers. The unofficial version was that he felt too overshadowed by Stack to continue in his role. Unlike Jerry Paris's exit from his Agent Flaherty role (he was just transferred to another office), George's departure wasn't to be so tidy: his Agent Cam Allison got bumped off in 'The Frank Nitti Story' episode.

Mid-April saw Charles Russell wind up his producing chores on the series and depart to start his own independent production company. At the end of May, Lloyd Richards, the production manager, was promoted to associate producer of *The Untouchables* for the 1960–61 season. Richards was a former production manager for the Western series *The Adventures of Jim Bowie* (ABC, 1956–58), *Yancy Derringer* (CBS, 1958–59) and the drama *Man with a Camera* (ABC, 1958–60).

*

Alongside the earlier Emmy awards, other honours and nominations received by the series for the 1959–60 season included nominations for best-produced series of 1959 (producers Sidney Marshall, Norman Retchin, Charles Russell and Joseph Shaftel) by the Screen Producers Guild; the 1959 Television Films' Directorial Award ('The Jake Lingle Killing', director Tay Garnett, with Vincent McEveety as assistant) by the Directors' Guild of America; and a prize for best sound-edited TV series of 1959 by the Motion Picture Sound Editors' organisation.

*

Two relevant gangster-themed movie releases around this time were *Pay or Die* (AA, 1960), Allied Artists' exploitation follow-up to their top grosser *Al Capone*; and *Murder Inc.* (20th Century-Fox, 1960), a film about the crime syndicate professional killers Anastasia and Buchalter.

Pay or Die dealt with organised crime in New York during the early part of the century, and featured Ernest Borgnine as Lt Joseph Petrosino, head of a detective team known as the Italian Squad because their main targets were members of the notorious La Mano Nera – the 'Black Hand'. The screenplay closely followed much of the real-life Mafia-smashing activities of Petrosino in Manhattan's 'Little Italy', until his assassination by the Mafia during a trip to Sicily on 12 March 1909: 'With Petrosino dead American law enforcement lost sight of the Mafia for almost fifty years.'[14] Richard Wilson directed the Richard Collins and Bertram Millhauser screenplay. Some ten years earlier, Gene Kelly and J. Carrol Naish had starred in a similar story and setting, *The Black Hand* (MGM, 1950), directed by Richard Thorpe (father of Jerry Thorpe) from Luther Davis and Leo Townsend's story.

Released a couple of months later, in June 1960, *Murder Inc.* featured the

34

vicious machinations of Albert Anastasia (played by Howard I. Smith), Louis 'Lepke' Buchalter (David J. Stewart) and killer-turned-informer Abe 'Kid Twist' Reles (Peter Falk) as they used thugs and killers to shake down the New York garment district, trucking business and sundry other legitimate enterprises. This outfit later became known as Murder Inc. The suspicious death of Reles in 1941 is the stuff that gangland folklore is made of. While kept in the Half Moon Hotel in New York under round-the-clock 'protective' police custody, as a prime witness against Bugsy Siegel, he was found dead six floors below his open window at 7 a.m. The theory was that he 'fell' while trying to escape.

*

Perhaps the most appropriate conclusion to the first season came from Frank DeBlois, writing in *TV Guide* magazine (26 March 1960):

> A unique appeal of *The Untouchables* is that the hoods, torpedoes, molls and alky smugglers who people this show are highly consistent – both in action and in word. In practically every episode a gang leader winds up stitched to a brick wall and full of bullets, or face down in a parking lot (and full of bullets), or face up in a gutter (and still full of bullets), or hung up in an ice box, or run down in the street by a mug at the wheel of a big black Hudson touring car.

For good or bad, *The Untouchables* had become a part of the popular consciousness.

4 'The Untouchables': Seasons Two and Three (1960–61; 1961–62)

Following the summer hiatus, *The Untouchables* started preparing for its second year with the signing, late in June 1960, of Alan Armer as one of several new producers for the series (he was elevated to executive producer in June 1961). Held over as a producer from the first year was Joseph Shaftel, under executive producer Jerry Thorpe. Paul Picerni, who had played one of Capone's hoods in the *Desilu Playhouse* original, also came on board now as a regular member of Ness's team, Agent Lee Hobson. It would be Picerni's Hobson who would remain the longest in viewers' memories as the foremost of Ness's sidekicks for the remainder of the series. Steve London, as Agent Rossman, also joined the squad on a regular basis at the start of the second season.

Season two opened with Leonard Kantor's 'The Rusty Heller Story' on 13 October 1960 (Thursday, 9.30–10.30 p.m.), skilfully directed by Walter Grauman, and guest starring Elizabeth Montgomery in the title role, as a tough young southern hooker who pits opposing underworld elements against each other. It turned out to be one of the best episodes of the second season. It also gave Montgomery a well-deserved Emmy nomination for Outstanding Performance by an Actress in a Leading Role (she lost out to Judith Anderson in *Hallmark Hall of Fame*'s 'Macbeth'). Many in the industry thought that she should have won.

'Eliot Ness and *The Untouchables* started their second season on ABC TV with a bang bang bang,' declared *Variety* (19 October 1960):

> It was a bullet a minute climaxing in an old-fashioned gang war, with occasionally a fist fight for a breather, or a girl getting socked, or a guy getting his tongue cut out. By way of relieving the rough stuff, Elizabeth Montgomery oozed sex between skirmishes, in as sensual a portrait as video has offered in a long time.

The second episode of the season took Ness to the East coast again for the 'Jack "Legs" Diamond' story (20/10/60), written by Charles O'Neal (from a story by Harry Essex) and directed by John Peyser. Based in part on the life of Legs Diamond (the alias of bootlegger John Nolan), the action centres on an incident which involved the importation of a million dollars in dope, and its subsequent hijacking by Diamond (played by Steven Hill).

Again, television's Eliot Ness intruded into the historical domain of US attorney Thomas Dewey of New York. It was Dewey who, in August 1931, had tried Diamond for operating an illegal still. Diamond was convicted, fined $10,000 and jailed for four years. Four months later, while out on bail awaiting appeal, Diamond was murdered. Also featured in the story were Dutch Schultz (played by

'The Untouchables' squad of series two: (l. to r.) Abel Fernandez, Nick Georgiade, Paul Picerni and Robert Stack.

Lawrence Dobkin), Lucky Luciano (Robert Carricart) and Alice Diamond (Norma Crane).

'The Waxey Gordon Story' (10/11/60) saw Ness go after the top bootlegger of the 1930s, another mobster who had originally been nailed by Dewey. One-time dope-pedlar and labour racketeer, Waxey Gordon (with a suitably ferocious performance from Nehemiah Persoff), owned breweries, nightclubs and hotels. He backed Broadway shows, sent his children to the most expensive schools and spent $4,000 on books with leather binding (which he never read) for his private library. Dewey's investigation proved that Gordon had made $4.5 million in two years and paid only $2,010 in tax. The evidence sent Gordon to jail for ten years; he was convicted only five days before Prohibition was repealed.

Ness then became involved with kidnapping, the way it was in pre-Lindbergh Law days of 1932, in 'The Purple Gang' (1/12/60), a visually striking example of film noir on the small screen (photographed by Charles Straumer). Under Walter Grauman's direction, the sets, casting and camerawork, particularly the shadowy, low-key lighting, develop a quasi-naturalistic and threatening ambience. Guest star Steve Cochran took the role of the psychopathic yet savvy leader of the Purple Gang who decides to hold a Capone mob courier for ransom.

*

Filming on the second season's two-part episode, 'The Big Train', had started in mid-September 1960, with John Peyser directing William Spier's script for producer Joseph Shaftel. Its transmission, on 5 and 12 January 1961, would lead Desilu and *The Untouchables* into their next scrape with the authorities.

The plot of 'The Big Train' saw Capone's mob seal off an entire California town to spring 'Scarface' from the special train moving federal prisoners cross-country to the new federal penitentiary of Alcatraz in 1934. While the actual train transportation background was authentic, the underworld machinations to effect the escape of Capone came strictly from Spier's typewriter.

In the episode it is Ness who suggests the establishment of such a place as Alcatraz for high-profile prisoners, as well as the special train to take them there. The delightfully crazy idea of a small band of heavily armed gangsters sealing off a town (where the train was to switch tracks) in order to battle it out with the guards and release Capone was typical *Untouchables* action material. The exciting climactic battle, more the spirit of the OK Corral than the Roaring Twenties, saw a marching line of federal agents, their shotguns and machine-guns blazing, blast it out with the mobsters in the town's main street. The end of the sequence suggested that *all* of the gangsters had been shot to death. No prisoners taken here. The episode closed with a shot of Ness smugly observing a very disappointed Capone through the train window as it continues its journey to Alcatraz. One almost wished that Capone *had* made his escape.

Robert J. Schoenberg outlines the actual historical background to the establishing of Alcatraz:

> On 1 August 1933, President Roosevelt's attorney general, Homer S. Cummings, asked an aide to consider, 'Would it not be well to think of having a special prison . . . It would be in a remote place – on an island, or in Alaska, so that the persons incarcerated would not be in constant communication with friends outside.' A week later, [the US Justice Department] had picked a site.
>
> It squatted lonely in the bay, one and one-quarter miles off the north shore of San Francisco, ripped by six-to-nine-knot, fifty-one-degree tidal currents. In 1775, Spanish sailors who first saw it covered with roosting birds named it 'Isla de Alcatraces' – Island of Pelicans.[15]

In 1933, Alcatraz Island was a military prison, but in July 1934 the US Army moved out and in August the Federal Bureau of Prisons took over.

On Saturday night, 18 August 1934, Al Capone and fifty-two other Atlanta federal penitentiary prisoners were preparing for their journey to Alcatraz:

> The government would take no chances on escape attempts from within or rescues from outside. A special train had been shunted into the prison yard. The barred windows of its steel cars were covered with heavy wire mesh. The guns of guards in screened cages could sweep the length of the aisles. At five a.m. next day, the train chugged out of the prison yard, its fifty-three prisoners shackled to their seats. The train stopped at none of the usual stations, its progress uncharted except by phoned reports to Warden [James A.] Johnston.
>
> When [the train arrived at Alcatraz on the morning of 22 August and] all were counted and processed . . . and locked in, Warden Johnston wired Cummings the agreed code: FIFTY-THREE CRATES OF FURNITURE FROM ATLANTA RECEIVED IN GOOD CONDITION INSTALLED NO BREAKAGE.[16]

'The Big Train' (parts one and two), guest-starring Neville Brand (in another excellent performance as Capone), Bruce Gordon (as Frank Nitti) and James Westerfield, was later re-edited for TV feature release (running at 96 minutes) as *Alcatraz Express.*

No sooner had the first part of 'The Big Train' aired when the director of the Bureau of Prisons, James Bennett, registered a complaint. As *TV Guide* magazine (21 January 1961) recounted:

> The Bureau's director James V. Bennett took strong objection to the first part of 'The Big Train' ... [and] demanded that Part 2 be withheld and threatened to appeal to the FCC [Federal Communications Commission] and the Attorney General for 'immediate and appropriate action.' Fumed Bennett in a wire to ABC: 'The utterly fantastic portrayal of the circumstances of the transfer of Al Capone to Alcatraz are unworthy. Also, to picture honorable and courageous officers as venal and a public institution like the Atlanta Penitentiary as toadying to Capone is an unforgivable public disservice.'
>
> Bennett also wired 10 ABC stations he would oppose their license renewals if they aired the second instalment. All 10 ignored the warning.
>
> The FCC, playing it cool, said only that if a formal complaint from Bennett were filed, the stations would be asked for their comments and the Commission would then decide whether or not any FCC rules or regulations had been violated. ABC's contribution: an announcement at the end of the show stating that no reflection on the integrity of the Bureau was intended.

But then, towards the end of February 1961, Bennett hurled a fresh barrage of complaints against *The Untouchables*. He sent FCC chairman Frederick W. Ford a new, detailed rundown of his complaints against the two recent episodes, which he said cast unjust aspersions on federal penitentiary personnel:

> Bennett's indictment centered on the programme's portrayal of the transfer of Capone which, he said, was actually accomplished 'without incident, shootings, bribery or attempted bribery.' Yet, Bennett contended, the programme 'effectively conveyed the impression that the dramatized events were based on actual fact.' Moreover, he said, no mention of the transfer was made in the book by the late G-man Eliot Ness, and 'it is flagrant deception therefore to say that the broadcast was based on the book.' (*Variety*, 22 February 1961)

Desilu and *The Untouchables* managed to weather this minor storm. But there was more trouble brewing ...

*

Midway through the second season, a small war developed around *The Untouchables* and began raging on two fronts. The first, and perhaps the most obvious, concerned the amount of violence displayed in every episode of the series, as Paul Robert Coyle explains: 'Undeniably, *The Untouchables* probably stands as the single most violent show in television history. But could it have been otherwise and still have been true to its time frame, which *was* bloody and bullet-riddled?'[17] These sentiments were echoed by Quinn Martin: '*The Untouchables* was supposed to be violent, damn it, it was supposed to be violent.'[18]

On 22 October 1960, *TV Guide* published an article by noted psychiatrist Dr Frederic Wertham called 'Do You Really Like *The Untouchables*?', in which Wertham, once again in his career as the knight of public morals, attempted to rouse the nation to the dangers of the exploitation of violence and horror in the mass media:

> We have learned from the clinic and from history that violence in fiction and in fact are not two totally separate worlds. Sparks may fly from one to the other. Violence is not strength. If democracy does not do away with violence, violence may do away with democracy.

Although Wertham's alarmist views tended to border on the hysterical, his observations regarding *The Untouchables* were not completely unfounded:

> There is cruelty related to sex, which is sadism. And there is murder as merciless elimination without emotion. All these varieties are supplied in *The Untouchables*. Here's a catalogue [in part]: a gangster shoots gleefully with many shots a man held for ransom; a young girl is shot in the back and killed; while one man is lying down, another bears heavily on his throat with a booted foot; truck drivers are tied to a tree with hoods over their faces and shot; the camera relishes the agony of the dying – when a gangster breaks his legs the Untouchables enjoy the result; a gang chief whales a Federal agent viciously with a whip, and a girl who collaborated with the police is shown in attractive negligee being choked – and also shot, for good measure.

Dr Frederic Wertham MD, it should be noted, was sole psychiatric consultant to the Kefauver Senate subcommittee investigating crime, and author of the controversial 1953 publication *Seduction of the Innocent* which, during the early 1950s, created an unnecessary public panic about the horror-laden direction taken by juvenile comic books in America.

Toward the end of the series' second season, Robert Lewis Shayon, in a piece entitled 'The Irresponsibles' for *Saturday Review* (25 February 1961), echoed Wertham's alarmist sermons:

> I readily admit that, as TV's tension-builders go, *The Untouchables* brings about the high degree of suspension of disbelief necessary for the required sixty-minute illusion. It's just that this particular programme is the apotheosis of the horror-comic sadism that masquerades under the old Sunday supplement banner of 'When Justice Triumphed'. The 'good guys' are as unrelated to anything recognisably human as are the bad guys. The 'Feds' kill and the mobsters kill – the second for business, the first for the lusty, vengeful joy of killing.

Perhaps some of the fears and paranoia of these times were justified (it was after all the time of the Cold War, Khrushchev, Eisenhower/Kennedy, Castro, Cuba and the Senate Rackets Committee hearings), but Quinn Martin and *The Untouchables* did attract some unnecessary heat. One particular (infamous) Martin memo to a writer, demanding more 'action', became a rather unfortunate exhibit for the anti-violence lobby. It stated: 'I wish you would come up with a different device than running the man down with a car, as we have done this now in three different shows. I like the idea of sadism, but I hope we can come up with another approach to it.'

The second assault on *The Untouchables* was rooted in the controversy over the series' prominent use of Italian names and backgrounds for the onscreen gangsters, and the general use of ethnic slurs. However, once again, in view of its historical foundation in the underworld life and times of Chicago of the 1920s, how else could the series depict that era?

The row began in early February 1961 when a member of the House of Representatives, and spokesman for the Federation of Italian-American Democratic Organizations, Alfred E. Santangelo, and three other congressmen, Republicans Victor Anfuso, Peter Rodino and Joseph P. Addabbo, hauled ABC vice-presidents Thomas W. Moore and Alfred R. Schneider across the carpet in a meeting held in Washington DC. As *Variety* (8 February 1961) reported:

> All had gripes about the bad stigma the show rubs off on Americans of Italian descent. Santangelo said he told the ABC execs that the programme has been 'seriously injuring the good character and reputation of the great majority' of such citizens. Further, he said, the series 'greatly distorts history.'

The ABC executives finally agreed to two concessions: first, that each future episode should conclude with the statement, 'fictional and designated for entertainment'; and second, that the producers should take it easy on Italian-Americans as villains.

But then, from another quarter, came a second assault. Anthony ('Tough Tony') Anastasia, representing the New York longshoremen, joined in the picketing of ABC's New York headquarters on 9 March. 'He threatened to order longshoremen to stop handling the products of Liggett & Myers, *The Untouchables'* biggest sponsor,' reported *TV Guide*:

> As boss of the Brooklyn waterfront he is in a position to carry out his threat.
> The Italian-American federation, organizer of the demonstration, announced that it was launching a boycott of L & M products. 'I don't know Mr Anastasia,' said Santangelo. 'We didn't solicit his support. As an American he protested, as he has a right to do. I think L & M is afraid of Anastasia.'
> Four days later L & M revealed that next fall it would not renew sponsorship of *The Untouchables* and two other ABC series ... L & M's advertising agency denied that the boycott had prompted the pullout. The agency explained that ABC had crossed it up by assigning later, less desirable, time-periods to the three shows. (*TV Guide*, 25 March 1961)

Santangelo's group was still considering its planned boycott of L & M even though the sponsor had decided to withdraw from the series:

> Action follows decision ... by Judges S. Samuel DiFalco and Ferdinand Pecora, of the National Italian-American League to Combat Defamation, to okay future *Untouchables* so long as producer Desi Arnaz doesn't use more fictional Italian names in a negative way. Arnaz agreed, but Santangelo said that this was not enough, because as he told ABC TV last January he did not want the [series] to use real Italians either, so long as they were merely used in fictional situations. (*Variety*, 22 March 1961)

ABC president Oliver Treyz announced that the network had already recouped $8.5 million of the $9 or 10 million lost to ABC in L & M's move. *The Untouchables*, he said, would be back next season, fully sponsored. *TV Guide* reported on the deal that had been struck:

> On St Patrick's Day came peace. Desi Arnaz ... ABC and the chairman of the Italian-

41

American League ... agreed: (1) There will be no more fictional hoodlums with Italian names in future productions; (2) There will be more stress on the law-enforcement role of 'Enrico Rossi', Ness's right-hand man in the show; (3) There will be emphasis on the 'formidable influence' of Italian-American officials in reducing crime and emphasis on the 'great contributions' made to American culture by Americans of Italian descent. (*TV Guide*, 25 March 1961)

According to Robert Stack, in *Straight Shooting*:

Strange as it may seem, some of Chicago's more notorious hoods loved the show. They didn't see themselves as villains on the screen. They were curiously interested in the show's accuracy.

Mobsters who didn't like the show regarded its actors as belonging to the same category as chorus girls or ball players – as hired hands. They turned their wrath upon the sponsors and Desi Arnaz ... Desi received an anonymous phone call threatening to 'blow his brains out' if the programme wasn't withdrawn. One of our sponsors, Liggett & Myers Tobacco Co., also had its problems. They discovered that their cigarettes were left on docks all over the country. The head of the Longshoremen's union in New York was one of the Anastasia brothers, also numbered among our archcritics. Rumor had it that Liggett & Myers would continue to have shipping problems until they dropped *The Untouchables*. But we were so hot by then that other sponsors jumped in and we kept right on going.[19]

Despite the compromises made by Desilu and ABC, Stack recalls that the battle raged on, uniting such diverse figures as Frank Sinatra, Cardinal Spellman and J. Edgar Hoover:

All three men hated *The Untouchables*. Together with Senator John Pastore, the powerful chairman of the Senate Communications Subcommittee, Frank Sinatra and Cardinal Spellman objected to the large number of Italian gangsters on the programme. J. Edgar Hoover didn't think that the show was accurate in its depiction of the G-men. Senator Thomas Dodd opened a hearing by the Senate Subcommittee on Juvenile Delinquency. (Tom Moore of ABC had to appear three times as a witness.) If two government investigations weren't enough, Newton Minow, [the new] chairman of the Federal Communications Commission, decided to hold hearings of his own, devoted to the subject of violence.

A final, almost amusing, note on this absurd period is described in Coyne Steven Sanders and Tom Gilbert's book *Desilu*:

Despite the truce between Italian-American groups and ABC and Desilu, an enraged Frank Sinatra abruptly moved his production company off the Desilu-Gower lot to Samuel Goldwyn Studios. 'What started as a discussion about Italians on Desilu's TV series, *The Untouchables*, ended up close to fisticuffs,' said one observer, who noted that Arnaz inflamed the altercation by calling Sinatra a 'television failure'. *Variety* reported, 'Frank Sinatra and Desi Arnaz almost came to blows at Desi's Indian Wells Hotel when Frank looked him up after midnight to discuss the depicting of Italians as ruthless mobsters on the *Untouchables* programmes.' To make peace with the volatile singer, Desi made Sinatra a standing offer of $1 million to produce any film of his choice at Desilu. 'That's what I think of Frank's talent and ability to draw at the box office,' stated a conciliatory Arnaz.

*

As production wound its way toward the end of the second season, Jerry Thorpe was named as vice-president in charge of programming at Desilu, a new post created by Arnaz as part of the continuing reorganisation of the studio following the departure of Martin Leeds as executive vice-president in 1960. Thorpe would head programme development and act as creative supervisor of the studio. Up until then, Arnaz had undertaken the top creative decisions at the studio himself, leaving the business decisions to Leeds. In mid-April, Stuart Rosenberg was signed up as staff producer-director for *The Untouchables*; having directed five episodes during the second season, he was down to direct ten and produce three for the 1961–62 season. Del Reisman was hired by Arnaz at the end of April as story editor for the series, working directly under Thorpe; Reisman had been a story editor, then associate producer, on *Playhouse 90* and *The Twilight Zone* (CBS, 1959–64).

The penultimate episode of the second season was Curtis Kenyon and John Mantley's 'The Nick Acropolis Story' (1/6/61), ably directed by Don Medford, and guest-starring Lee Marvin as a gambling chief who challenges Nitti. An interesting point was raised in *The Hollywood Reporter* review (5 June 1961):

> The name of Frank Nitti is used; he is a pertinent character, wonderfully cruelly played by Bruce Gordon. There are some other names used which might lead ethnic and other groups to protest; the defense and the protest should be to make the impossible denial that they did not exist. Eliot Ness did, and so did they, either in fact or prototype, although the alibi disclaimer is that 'certain portions of this episode were fictionalized'.

With all the trials and traumas of the 1960–61 season, both Desilu and ABC must have been delighted when *TV Guide* magazine asked Eliot Ness's widow, Elisabeth, to write a piece about the series and her late husband. Entitled 'My Husband Eliot Ness' (11 March 1961), Mrs Ness was full of praise for the series:

> I am very happy about Mr Stack's interpretation of the role. He has the same quietness of voice, the same gentle quality that characterized Eliot. At times, even Stack's small mannerisms are similar. He smiles less, but Mr Stack has been given less to laugh at than Eliot found in real life.
>
> I like the programme and I wouldn't miss it, even though I no longer know what it will be about. It is fiction, the stories are not of what Eliot was doing at that time. But since they are, in spirit, the same – the enforcement of law and order, the fight against exploitation of the law-abiding members of society, the hunting down of criminals – Eliot's admirers should not feel let down.
>
> The true stories, what he was doing, are just as exciting as the fiction that you see.

*

The Untouchables' second season had spawned a number of series on a similar theme, including: *The Witness* (CBS, 1960–61), which promised to reveal history by conducting congressional-type hearings of such notorious figures as Lucky Luciano, Bugsy Siegel and Legs Diamond; Warner Bros' *The Roaring 20's* (ABC, 1960–62), a newspaper-reporter series set in New York City in the 1920s; and MGM's *The Asphalt Jungle* (ABC, 1961), a contemporary police detective drama featuring an Untouchables-like group of crimefighters. *The Lawless Years* reappeared for a final, brief stint during the summer months (May–September) of 1961.

The Warner Bros television series *The Roaring 20's* tried to emulate *The Untouchables* style of action (as seen here in the 1961 episode 'The Maestro').

On the theatrical-release side, Joseph Pevney's *Portrait of a Mobster* (WB, 1961), following up on the studio's *The Rise and Fall of Legs Diamond* of the previous year, featured Vic Morrow as Dutch Schultz. The film opened in March 1961 and, according to *Variety* (29 March 1961), was ensured a 'respectable, if short-lived, boxoffice showing'. Also appearing in the story were Vincent Coll, played by Evan McCord, and Legs Diamond, with Ray Danton re-creating his 1960 role. *Mad Dog Coll* (Columbia, 1961), directed by Burt Balaban and starring John Davis Chandler in the title role, appeared in May 1961 and was regarded as 'a one-dimensional study' (by *The Hollywood Reporter* (3 May 1961)) of the early 1930s killer. David Janssen starred as grand crime kingpin Arnold Rothstein in the June release of *King of the Roaring 20's* (AA, 1961; subtitled *The Story of Arnold Rothstein*). 'Commercially, the Allied Artists release will go only so far as thorough exploitation can take it, which doesn't figure to be too far,' reckoned *Variety* (21 June 1961).

*

Preparing for *The Untouchables'* third season, in May 1961, Robert Stack told *The Hollywood Reporter* (16 May 1961):

> A year ago I said that when my three-year contract [for the series] was up, I'd quit being Ness for good. Now, I'm not too sure – I might go along, if they decide to go a fourth season. Mind you, even Desilu won't know till we're well into our third season this fall.

44

Stack's inference was that he was more enthusiastic about the series than ever, and not just about his role but the efforts of all concerned with the production. 'We're trying to make our third season the best yet,' he added. 'We're only shooting 26 instead of the usual 32 segments in an effort to make every one a quality hour – and we'll be working as long and as hard, if not longer and harder, as we did last year.' At the same time Stack advised his agents that he would not be able to take on any feature-film assignments for another year, which would include his own Langford Productions' US Navy feature project *Hide and Seek* (unrealised).

*

The third season (1961–62), which had begun production in July, opened with Louis Peletier's 'The Troubleshooter' (12/10/61; with Peter Falk as a New York hood imported by the Chicago underworld to tackle Ness), the broadcast date of which, ironically enough, was 12 October 1961 – Columbus Day! Obviously, things were cooling down on the defamation front.

By way of notable episodes, the third season had been by now so watered-down in terms of action ('violence') and historical background ('Italian gangster types') that an obvious blandness had set in. And it showed on the screen. For the most part, the bad guys in the scripts were of a distinctly WASP origin; although a few instances of characters with German-sounding names nearly brought the German-Americans into the complaints department.

'The Genna Brothers' (2/11/61), featuring Marc Lawrence and Antony Carbone as Mike and Angelo Genna, respectively, was among the very few episodes based on real-life characters seen during the third season. Of the six 'terrible' Genna brothers of early 1920s Chicago, Michael and Angelo were the gang's tough enforcers who kept their illegal stills going in the Little Italy district of the city. They installed crude stills in hundreds, eventually thousands, of tenement flats, houses and spare rooms throughout Little Italy:

> The Gennas sold spirits made of home-cooked mash blended with flavours and colouring, achieving instantly what took years in genuine whiskey. In went creosote, coal-tar dyes, fusel oil and wood alcohol which could kill the drinker in less than an hour.[20]

A later episode, 'Arsenal' (28/6/62), written by John Mantley and directed by Paul Wendkos, involved Ness in a gang war when Chicago hoods discover there is no local, state or federal law making the sale of machine-guns illegal.

The first recorded use in Chicago of a sub-machine-gun, in September 1925, had heralded a new epoch in Chicago gang warfare. The co-invention of former army officer and Remington Arms Corporation employee John T. Thompson, the .45 calibre 'tommy gun' or 'chopper', as it soon became known, was designed for use by US troops during the First World War. However, the Armistice was signed before Thompson's Auto-Ordnance company could supply the guns to the Army. In 1923, Auto-Ordnance dropped its price of the weapon from $225 to $175, but by 1925 it had sold only around three thousand guns:

> The world was ignoring quite a weapon. Stripped, it weighed eight and a half pounds; fully configured, with stock and a hundred-round drum, the weight rose to a little over twenty pounds – still perfectly manageable. Its rate of fire was one thousand rounds a

Neville Brand as 'Scarface' Al Capone – the first of his only two appearances in *The Untouchables*

minute, and each round could punch through quarter-inch steel plate. . . . No one then needed a permit to own or carry a submachine gun, which could be bought through sporting goods firms, hardware stores or by mail order.[21]

*

In early April 1961, former *Untouchables* producer Charles Russell was named as producer on MGM TV's new *Cain's Hundred* series, created by Paul Monash (who would also act as executive producer). Prior to the series' première, the New York Italian-Defamation group embarrassed themselves when they called upon NBC, believing that *Cain's Hundred* might have an *Untouchables* slant. NBC screened the pilot episode for them to prove that the only Italian in the show was a 'good guy' district attorney.

Cain's Hundred (NBC, 1961–62), about an underworld lawyer who turns on his former employers when they kill his fiancée, closely resembled *The Untouchables*, despite its contemporary setting.

This was just one of the three 1961–62 season series that attempted to emulate *The Untouchables'* popularity.

Next came John Burrows and Leonard Ackerman's *Target: The Corruptors* (ABC, 1961–62), a crusading newspaper-columnist series filmed in a stark monochrome style. The show was based on (creator and story consultant) Lester Velie's series of published crime exposés indicting contemporary criminals who prey on an only passively concerned public.

In October 1960, Quinn Martin's new independent company had announced the production of *The New Breed* (ABC, 1961–62), a series based on the activities of the Metropolitan Squad of the LA Police Department. It was clearly another *Untouchables*, but for the modern day, and represented Quinn Martin's attempt, on the insistence of ABC, to reprise his *Untouchables'* success.

*

The final gangster feature-film release for this period was Joseph M. Newman's *The George Raft Story* (AA, 1961) in late November 1961. Ray Danton starred as Raft in this rather shallow portrait of the notorious actor-dancer. 'One of the film's more interesting vignettes,' said *Variety* (6 December 1961), 'is the scene in which Raft, following his success in *Scarface*, is summoned to the Chicago headquarters of Al Capone, portrayed once again by Neville Brand, who is making something of a career-within-a-career of portraying the character.'

In 1962, Arnaz and programming vice-president Jerry Thorpe announced plans to produce several television pilots for the upcoming 1962–63 season (mostly in the vein of musical-comedies and domestic comedy series), as well as an intriguing theatrical feature, *The Story of Eliot Ness*, in which Robert Stack would reprise his *Untouchables* role. Sadly, that was the last that was heard of the idea.

5 'The Untouchables': Season Four (1962–63) and After . . .

On 6 March 1962, following rumours that the series was drawing to a close, the ABC network announced 'officially' that *The Untouchables* would go to a fourth year. Toward the end of 1961, everyone, including ABC and Desilu, had been mulling over whether to pursue a fourth season in view of the series' recent problems, many of which remained active with the continuing Senate 'sex and violence' probe. Senator Thomas J. Dodd and his juvenile delinquency subcommittee were still charging the three networks with deliberately injecting more sex and violence into their TV shows to boost ratings.

At the end of the third season, Robert Stack (whose three-year contract had expired) had agreed to continue as Ness for a fourth year if Desilu bought out his 25 per cent interest in the series for the minimum of a million dollars. In a highly complex proposed deal, Langford Productions would receive $1 million plus – contingent on his playing Ness for two more years.

Leonard Freeman joined the series as the new executive producer in early April 1962, replacing Alan Armer who was departing to produce his own show. Freeman had come from his producer role on Lancer Productions' *Route 66* (CBS, 1960–64) at Screen Gems. Also joining *The Untouchables* for the fourth season was veteran TV producer Alvin Cooperman (who, incidentally, had been a part of the team who had devised colour TV for FCC approval in 1953); Cooperman would resign as producer in January 1963 in order to move to New York. Newscaster Les Lampson, the regular announcer (over the opening titles and credits) for the past three years, was retained for a fourth year, which meant that he had a seven-day weekly work schedule, since he also continued his KTTV weekend newscasts on Saturdays and Sundays.

Just prior to the 5 July start of production, Freeman and Cooperman moved their offices from Desilu-Gower, where *The Untouchables* had been produced from the beginning, over to the Desilu-Culver studios (the old Pathé studio in Culver City).

July–August also saw a reshuffle in the series' music department. On 24 July it was announced that Henry Mancini had been signed up to score two episodes; this was followed a week later by the news that Pete Rugolo would score a further two episodes; and on 23 August it was revealed that Leith Stevens, in a multiple deal, would compose the scores for six episodes. All of this under Desilu's new music scoring concept for *The Untouchables* which would call on at least ten top composers to create original scores during the fourth season.

The fourth, and what would be the final, season of *The Untouchables* opened

Robert Stack as Eliot Ness.

with Mort Thaw's 'The Night They Shot Santa Claus' episode on 25 September 1962 (Tuesday, 9.30–10.30 p.m.; previously, the series had been broadcast on Thursday nights). The story, in which Ness unravels the threads of the dual life led by a man killed by gangsters, reflected the season's new format: it was now intended that Stack's Eliot Ness would show a more human, vulnerable side, as well as be seen to lose some of his crime-busting cases. At the conclusion of this first episode, Ness, as usual, nails the murderer, but the suspect is acquitted. All the witnesses were dead.

Also, replacing the style of the previous standard pre-credits action scenes, the new episodes began with the opening of *The Untouchables* book cover (with title logo) revealing a page inscribed with 'The Untouchables 1929–1933', followed by a second page that gave the particular episode title above a freeze-frame image of the opening scene. The intention, presumably, was to emphasise the show's book-based 'accuracy'. The new end-titles disclaimer now stated: 'The incidents portrayed in this episode are fictional, although certain of the characterizations are based upon the book "The Untouchables" by Eliot Ness and Oscar Fraley.'

Another change in the presentation of the fourth season's *Untouchables* was the inclusion of 'back-door' pilot spin-offs (new characters introduced in regular episodes with the intention of setting them up in their own series). Usually the sign of a wilting series. A major factor behind this latter development was the return of Lucille Ball to regular television in *The Lucy Show* (CBS, 1962–74). This half-hour sitcom, much in the slapstick style of the old *I Love Lucy* shows, became an immediate ratings winner and prompted Desilu (now headed by Ball) to announce 'a sum conservatively estimated at $1,000,000' for the production of 1963–64 pilots.

There would be three potential series spin-off pilots derived from *The Untouchables*.

*

The first pilot deveoped from the episode 'Bird in the Hand' (30/10/62), written by Harry Kronman and directed by Walter Grauman, guest-starring Dane Clark, Joseph Schildkraut and John Gabriel as a public health medical team. The story described how Ness tracks a small-time hoodlum from Chicago to Washington DC, to find that the Health Department is also interested in the case (the medical aspect concerned a rare bird disease that was also contagious to humans). The intended spin-off series was to be called *The White Knight*: set in the early 1930s, it was based on the then urgent need for an adequate US Public Health service.

A second pilot was filmed (shooting began in December 1962) and shown as 'Jake Dance' (22/1/63), with Robert Butler directing Gilbert Ralston's story about Ness engineering a jail delivery to free a mobster who can lead him to the head of the ring which has been flooding Chicago with poisoned liquor. Clark, Schildkraut and Gabriel once again guest-starred, with Stack's Ness relegated to the sidelines of the plot.

The 'Jake dance' was a rather cruel street term for a terminally crippling side-effect (paralysis) that came with the consumption of synthetic Jamaica Ginger, a cheap whiskey substitute commonly known as Ginger Jake. The infamous 'hooch' had also featured in a second-season bootlegging episode called, of course, 'The Jamaica Ginger Story' (2/2/61).

Had it sold, *The White Knight* would have been the first non-contemporary medical series among the then popular trend that included the *Dr Kildare* (NBC, 1961–66) and *Ben Casey* (ABC, 1961–66) hospital series.

*

In September 1962, Barbara Stanwyck had been signed up by Desilu to star in two episodes of *The Untouchables* to be developed as pilots for a new one-hour series titled *The Seekers*. The first of these to be broadcast was 'Elegy' (20/11/62), from a script by Herman Groves and Harold Gast, and directed by Robert Butler. When a dying gangster asks for Ness's help in locating his missing daughter, Ness calls on

Lt Aggie Stewart (Stanwyck) of the Missing Persons' Bureau of the Chicago Police Department for assistance.

The second *Seekers* pilot, 'Search for a Dead Man' (1/1/63; originally titled 'Flowers for My Love'), followed Stanwyck's Lt Stewart as she tried to uncover the identity of a corpse floating in Lake Michigan. Again, director Butler and writers Groves and Gast provided the words and images.

Unfortunately, these Stanwyck pilots were overly talky and slow-moving, following the step-by-step paces of the central characters as they conducted their missing persons' investigations. Nearly every dialogue exchange was loaded with (1930s) facts and details, reflective of the 1950s *Dragnet* procedurals. Presenting little or no action, they were almost the opposite of all that *The Untouchables'* firepower represented. Not surprisingly, the expected *Seekers* series failed to materialise.

'The Floyd Gibbons Story' (11/12/62) was the only *Untouchables* pilot completely controlled by Stack's Langford Productions company, but still produced in partnership with Desilu. Also known as 'Floyd Gibbons: Reporter', the episode featured an abrasive, eye-patched Scott Brady as the real-life globe-trotting newspaperman, correspondent and commentator Floyd Gibbons (whose actual 1916–39 adventures included being captured by Pancho Villa and losing an eye in the Second Battle of the Marne).

In *The Untouchables* episode, the famed war correspondent helps Ness solve the slaying of a reporter friend and uncover an underworld operation in which the mob are secretly exporting munitions metal to Japan and Germany. George Eckstein's teleplay, while mainly focusing on Gibbons's purported 1932 Chicago gangland adventure, also gave Brady and co-star Dorothy Malone (as the victim's tragic widow) a profoundly potent reunion scene which appeared to suggest that they had (perhaps adulterously) exchanged emotional sparks in the past. Despite the episode's dramatic thrust, under Robert Butler's rather restrained direction, *The World of Floyd Gibbons*, as the series was to be called, was not picked up by the network.

The close of this period was recounted by Coyne Steven Sanders and Tom Gilbert:

> Desilu executive Ed Holly admitted that the studio had experienced recent financial problems: 'We tightened our belts and cut four hundred thousand dollars from the overhead.' As one example, to cut $20,000 per-episode union penalties and overtime costs resulting from expensive evening filming, *The Untouchables* began shooting night-time scenes during less-costly daytime hours by placing black muslin over camera lenses.

Unfortunately, not all of the show's problems were so easily solved; the series had sparked hearings by the FCC and congressional committees:

> Responding to such criticism and forced to tamper with the show's solid success, Arnaz brought aboard *Route 66* producer Leonard Freeman. The new executive producer vowed that *The Untouchables* would be devoid of 'violence without motivation.' ... Robert Stack heatedly objected to the many changes imposed upon the series: 'The criticism of *The Untouchables* is a paradox – it's because the show is successful. If it weren't, there'd be no need to criticize.'

The toned-down *Untouchables* perhaps satisfied members of the FCC and an ongoing Senate probe on excessive television violence, but appealed to few viewers. As ratings for the once top-ranked show plummeted, Arnaz moved swiftly and returned the crime drama to its original successful formula. 'I don't like violence for violence's sake,' Desi insisted. 'I don't think *The Untouchables* originally had too much violence, because we are portraying an era of violence.' ... Answering the charge that the programme also displayed excessive erotica, Arnaz countered, 'I don't think there is too much sex on TV – I don't think there's *any.*'[22]

Leonard Freeman left the series after only thirteen episodes.

*

In late January 1963, the Hollywood trade papers announced that Stack's Langford Productions had been acquired by Desilu Productions through a stock-exchange deal, in which Stack received 77,691 Desilu shares. At the market value, the payment to Stack was approximately $600,000. Langford, however, would continue producing the series. If the show was not picked up for a fifth year, it would be put into immediate syndication. *The Untouchables* had grossed nearly $1 million to date.

*

Then came the day. On Friday 29 March 1963, after four years of production, *The Untouchables* wound up the fourth season's final episode. As *The Hollywood Reporter* (26 March 1963) announced: 'Mobsters and Feds will bury the hatchet Sunday night in the Valley's Casa Escober [restaurant] when Bob Stack hosts a wake for *The Untouchables.*' In what may serve as a fitting conclusion to the four years of the original series, Gilbert Seldes, reviewing for *TV Guide* (29 September 1962) observes:

> The usual TV crime show doesn't particularly care whether you believe it in detail. *The Untouchables* has three items working for credibility: the voice of Walter Winchell, which is absolutely right – it comes at you in bursts like a machine gun; the manner of Robert Stack as Ness – the organization man as a crime-fighter, efficient and without heroics; and the underlying fact that while the show deals with a crime or a series of crimes, in each episode, it is really about the organization of crime – the corporate structure that plans and executes crime, the wholesaler for whom the gunman does the dirty work.

For Gianakos: 'Ness triumphs only in the physical sense, but the cesspool triumphs spiritually.'

The third great TV and movie gangster cycle was over. A brief Second World War television trend (*Combat!*, *The Gallant Men*, *McHale's Navy*) soon gave way to the exceptionally popular TV and movie spy/espionage genre that would go on to dominate the decade. However, a few worthwhile gangster features managed to trickle through during the remainder of the 1960s – the youthful exploitation programmer *Young Dillinger* (AA, 1965), Roger Corman's beautifully crafted *The St Valentine's Day Massacre* (20th Century-Fox, 1967) and the violently happy-go-lucky crime spree of *Bonnie and Clyde* (WB, 1967) – before Paramount's *The Godfather* breathed new life into the (cinema) genre in 1972.

The Untouchables (Para, 1987): Kevin Costner as Eliot Ness with Sean Connery as Officer Jim Malone.

Kevin Costner and director Brian DePalma attempted to return to the 1950s book source (from a screenplay by David Mamet) and the 1920s setting with the June 1987 release of *The Untouchables* (Paramount). While the texture of the film is a tribute to the work of art director William A. Elliott (the La Salle Street exteriors, for instance), the unfortunate depiction of Costner's Ness as a latent homicidal maniac, De Niro's Capone as an underworld prima donna and the Frank Nitti character (played well enough by Billy Drago) as a rampant psychopath is at times quite absurd, even laughable. For the late 1980s, DePalma should have known better.

Perhaps inspired by the one-shot box-office success of the Costner–DePalma film, Eliot Ness was back on the small screen in a 'revisit' television special. *The Return of Eliot Ness* (NBC, 10/11/91) starred Robert Stack in this 120-minute telefeature, filmed on location in Toronto by Michael Filerman Productions and set in a makeshift post-Second World War Chicago. Co-producer Michael Petryni's script saw Ness coming out of retirement to clear the name of a murdered colleague (a former Untouchable). *Daily Variety* (8 November 1991) summed it up:

> Unfortunately, every plot twist and turn is telegraphed to viewers, leaving the climactic violent conclusion a foregone one. Despite his character's limitations, Stack has enough credibility to pull off the role. The other cast members [Jack Coleman, Philip Bosco, Charles Durning] also seem to have fun with their parts, which helps salvage the stale script. The inclusion of some old footage of postwar Chicago also helps the film along, as does the mood-setting music of the era from Lee Holdridge.

Two years later, *The Untouchables* returned as a remade first-run syndicated series (January–May 1993, eighteen one-hour episodes plus a two-hour pilot; October 1993–April 1994, twenty-six one-hour episodes) produced by

The Untouchables (Para, 1987): Kevin Costner's Eliot Ness during a brewery raid.

Christopher Crowe Productions in association with Paramount Network TV. Television newcomer Tom Amandes featured as a rather tepid Eliot Ness, with veteran screen tough William Forsythe as a fierce Al Capone. The two-hour début episode traced the childhoods of Ness and Capone, and how their paths came to cross in Chicago. The series was filmed in Chicago locations and at Chicago Studio City.

Unlike the original series, this updated version picked up the Capone–Ness story before the mobster was convicted and was therefore able to depict the appropriate period, places and people. Jeff Jarvis, reviewing in *TV Guide* (30 January 1993), had this to say:

> TV's latest remake of a remake of the story of mobster Al Capone versus G-man Eliot Ness is often laughably sincere (Ness on his nemesis: 'Damn him! How in the name of God did the world ever get visited by a monster like this?'). If Mickey Rooney made a mobster movie, it would sound like this. But it wouldn't look like this. The series is lavishly, impressively made.

However, by the second series the show was exhibiting signs of strain, with some trade observers regarding it as 'decidedly non-violent' and that it 'anachronistically falters occasionally in the dialogue department'. Tony Scott, reviewing for *Variety* (11 October 1993), was forced to comment: 'For a story about the breakup of a crime syndicate whose fortunes were made on bootlegging, prostitution and gambling, the [first episode of series two] is squeaky clean.'

*

With the Capone case concluded, the real-life Untouchables were disbanded and Eliot Ness was made Chief Investigator of Prohibition Forces for the entire Chicago division, in recognition of his work.

In 1933, the FBI moved him to Cincinnati to clean up the moonshiners of Kentucky, Tennessee and Ohio, where he confiscated hundreds of hillbilly stills. Ness was subsequently assigned to the Northern District of Ohio as investigator in charge of the Treasury Department's Alcoholic Tax Unit. When Cleveland elected a reform ticket in 1935, Ness was asked to direct an investigation of police department corruption. He became the city's Director of Public Safety, and, over a period of some six years, forced two hundred resignations and sent a dozen high officers to the state prison. During that time, he established the Cleveland Police Academy and reorganised the traffic bureau.

From 1941 to 1945, Ness served as Director of Social Protection for the Federal Security Agency. After the Second World War, he moved his family (wife Betty and their eleven-year-old son Bobby) to Pennsylvania, where he became president of the Guaranty Paper Corporation and Fidelity Check Corporation.

Eliot Ness died on 16 May 1957.

In January 1939, after five years in the federal prison, Al Capone was transferred from Alcatraz and shuttled through a series of government institutions before being formally released in November 1939.

Now diagnosed as presenting the classics symptoms of paresis, having originally been examined for syphilis at Atlanta penitentiary in 1932, Capone had deteriorated mentally.

Accompanied by his family, Capone moved to his Florida home, where he lingered on for seven years, often delirious and abstracted. His condition steadily worsened until finally he suffered a brain haemorrhage followed by pneumonia.

His death came from cardiac arrest on 25 January 1947.

*

The Untouchables 'was the precursor of a type of quality rarely achieved on television in those days', recalled Robert Stack in his autobiography. 'Its crudity and violence might amuse or infuriate viewers today; but, for its time, it was a remarkable show.'

The third great Gangster film and TV cycle may have gone but the original *The Untouchables* is still in syndication on the international market (distributed by Paramount Television; also in French, German, Japanese, Portuguese and Spanish language versions). After some thirty-five years, *The Untouchables* still stands as the greatest sequence of gangster movies ever made for the small screen – all 118 hours of them.

Why?

Because devils are usually far more fascinating than saints.

Notes

1. Brooks Robards, 'The Police Show', in Brian G. Rose (ed.), *TV Genres* (Westport, CT: Greenwood Press, 1985), p. 12.
2. Malvin Wald, 'The Making of a Bio-Pic', *Films in Review*, April 1959, p. 16.
3. Larry James Gianakos, *Television Drama Series Programming: 1959–1975* (Metuchen, NJ: The Scarecrow Press, 1978), p. 261.
4. Coyne Steven Sanders and Tom Gilbert, *Desilu* (New York: William Morrow, 1993), pp. 173–74.

 5. *Ibid.*, p. 174.
 6. *Ibid.*, p. 175.
 7. Neal Gabler, *Walter Winchell: Gossip, Power and the Culture of Celebrity* (London: Basingstoke: Picador, 1995), p. 508.
 8. Robert Stack with Mark Evans, *Straight Shooting* (New York: Macmillan, 1980), p. 207.
 9. Robert J. Schoenberg, *Mr Capone* (London: Robson Books, 1992), p. 308.
10. Stack with Evans, *Straight Shooting*, p. 218.
11. Schoenberg, *Mr Capone*, pp. 358–59.
12. Gianakos, *Television Drama Series Programming: 1959–1975*, pp. 261–62.
13. Schoenberg, *Mr Capone*, p. 359.
14. Martin Short, *Crime Inc.* (London: Thames Methuen, 1984), p. 32.
15. Schoenberg, *Mr Capone*, p. 334.
16. *Ibid.*, p. 335.
17. Paul Robert Coyle, 'The Untouchables', *Emmy*, July 1984, p. 68.
18. Horace Newcomb and Robert S. Alley, *The Producer's Medium* (Oxford: Oxford University Press, 1983), p. 67.
19. Stack with Evans, *Straight Shooting*, pp. 218–19.
20. Short, *Crime Inc.*, p. 79.
21. Schoenberg, *Mr Capone*, p. 141.
22. Sanders and Gilbert, *Desilu*, pp. 230–31.

PART TWO

Robert Stack's Ness crashing into gangland, again.

Epilog One: The American Gangster Film Cycle

Since *The Untouchables* assumes that we are already familiar with gangsters and gangster films, any discussion of the series must begin with an examination of the gangster film. Also, because the gangster film is such a wide-ranging genre, it may help to identify its chief components. Gangster films are not necessarily films about gangsters but invariably use the organised criminal underworld as a basis for their fictional narrative; the gangland element, though it may be in the background, still remains the *raison d'être* for a gangster film story. The gangster film is a well-documented American genre, rich in iconography and populated by well-defined gangster variants such as the bootlegger, the racketeer and the hired killer, as well as the complementary characters of the wise-cracking moll, the cigar-chewing kingpin, the shyster lawyer, the crooked cop and the snivelling stool-pigeon.

Subdivisions of the genre include the semi-documentary-styled G-man films, various prison, boxing and exposé films, gangster biographies, caper films, rural/Depression-era gangster features and syndicate or Mafia films, alongside the multiple elements of film noir. Between the 1920s and the late 1950s the gangster film evolved through two major cycles and various phases (the latter generally categorised via the above subdivisions). *The Untouchables*, as a television series comprising 118 hour-long stories, reached back and employed most of the cinema's gangster themes, icons and variants for its retelling of Prohibition times. In so doing, the series helped create the third major gangster film cycle (1959 to 1963).

This new cycle developed from two significant factors: the March 1959 release of Allied Artists' *Al Capone* (which broke almost all existing box-office records on its release across America, especially in Chicago) and the April 1959 television presentation of Desilu's two-parter, 'The Untouchables' (which achieved an audience rating of 36.1 per cent).[1] It may be one of those bizarre coincidences that both happened to be period biographies set in the same place (Chicago) during the same time (Prohibition) and concerning the same subject (Al Capone). In a sense it represented a true cycle, a full circle of the characters and events that originally gave birth to the genre.

The world of the organised urban gangster as a film subject did not develop until the latter part of the 1920s, although an early appearance of the urban criminal on the screen can be traced back to D. W. Griffith's 1912 *The Musketeers of Pig Alley*. The period of films that began with the release of Josef von Sternberg's *Underworld* (Paramount) and moved through to Howard

G-Men (WB, 1935): James Cagney, flanked by Lloyd Nolan, on the side of the law for a change.

G-Men (WB, 1935): FBI man James Cagney in the hands of the mob.

Hawks's *Scarface* (UA) – 1927 to 1932 – is generally regarded by historians as the first great gangster film cycle. Andrew Sarris neatly and conveniently subtitled this early part of the genre as 'the gangster as subjective protagonist and romantic hero'.[2] The standard textbook titles of notable gangster films for this period include *Little Caesar* (WB, 1930), *The Public Enemy* (WB, 1931), *City Streets* (Paramount, 1931), *Doorway to Hell* (WB, 1930) and *Quick Millions* (Fox, 1931). And, perhaps, the titles tell it all. But after just five years the new genre appeared to be over, concluding, ironically, with the onscreen demise of Paul Muni's Tony Camonte (in *Scarface*) as he is gunned down under a travel-shop window sign declaring 'The World Is Yours'.

The actual demise of the genre can be attributed to the increasing agitation against the gangster film: from the censors over the glorification of gangsters and violence on the screen; and from such formidable pressure groups as the American Legion, the Daughters of the American Revolution, as well as from various big-business interests (gangster film stories often portrayed powerful businessmen as being in league with the mob). That a similar fate would befall *The Untouchables* some thirty years later is perhaps more sad than sinister.

However, just a couple of years later, the gangster film returned intact with all the action, violence and corruption associated with the genre. But this time the genre projected a manifest difference. No longer was the gangster the 'tragic hero' in the Tony Camonte mould. He had become a government man, a dedicated lawman on the other side of the fence. William Keighley's *G-Men* (WB, 1935) was perhaps the first notable entry in this new gangster cycle, where the emphasis shifted from 'the unmaking of a criminal to the making of a G-Man'.[3] In *G-Men*, James Cagney, who only a few years earlier had risen to gangland heights in *Public Enemy*, had become an FBI agent who uses the same ruthless tactics against mobsters as he had previously employed against rival gangsters. The following year, Keighley's *Bullets or Ballots* (WB) featured Edward G. Robinson as a New York cop smashing a racketeer syndicate by infiltrating the mob as a disgraced ex-policeman. Among the other FBI-inspired,[4] racket-busting films to appear during this time were Sam Wood's *Let 'Em Have It* (Reliance Pictures, 1935; a Department of Justice showcase), J. Walter Rubin's *Public Hero Number One* (MGM, 1935; with G-man Chester Morris tracking down a mobster kingpin), and Alexander Hall's *I Am the Law* (Columbia, 1938; with Edward G. Robinson's DA fighting corrupt city government). Fortunately, the decade drew to a close with two extraordinary gangster film productions that harked back to the beginning of the genre; both were set around the rise and fall of a gangster in Prohibition-era style, and both starred James Cagney.

The first, *Angels With Dirty Faces* (WB, 1938), was reflected spiritually in *The Untouchables'* view of the urban underworld, with its lusty melodramatics and its representation of the gangster as a self-destructive character who is caught up in a grinding system from which there is no escape. Cagney's defiant Rocky Sullivan character, a man too deeply embedded in the machinations of the mob to survive on either side of the law, is replayed in multiple characterisations in *The Untouchables*: for example, the character played by Harold J. Stone in 'The Tommy Karpeles Story' (29/12/60); by Harry Guardino in 'The Nick Moses Story'

The Roaring Twenties (WB, 1939): James Cagney in classic gangster form.

(23/2/61); by Peter Falk in 'The Troubleshooter' (12/10/61); by Telly Savalas in 'The Speculator' (8/1/63); and by Paul Richards in 'City without a Name' (14/12/61) – all of whom try to buck the system of both organised crime and organised law enforcement. However, unlike the Cagney character, all of the *Untouchables* gangsters bring about their own downfall (usually in a violent manner) through the usual excesses of personal greed for wealth and/or power; and, unlike the fate of Rocky Sullivan (in the end, a bad man gone good), we feel not the slightest regret at their passing.

While *Angels with Dirty Faces* and other post-1935 gangster films were presented as contemporary, Raoul Walsh's *The Roaring Twenties* (WB, 1939) was the first major gangster film to actually set its story during Prohibition, thus making it the first 'period' gangster film.

The rise and fall of Cagney's 'big shot' gangster Eddie Bartlett mirrors the real-life career of New York club owner and gangster Larry Fay.[5] Mark Hellinger's story traces Bartlett's racketeering career from small-time bootlegger to powerful gang boss during the hysterical years of Prohibition and the speakeasies of the early 1920s that evolved into the plush nightclubs which festooned New York's Broadway in the years leading up to the stock-market crash and the Great Depression: ultimately, the story of a good man gone bad. *Roaring Twenties'* careful use of newsreel footage to convey the Prohibition decade, as well as the film's keen observation of correct period clothes, cars, jazz-age music and interior and exterior settings, set it immediately apart from contemporary gangster films. In 1959, Desilu and producer Quinn Martin would achieve similar results, albeit on a much smaller scale, in their television reconstruction of the period (though *The Untouchables'* second-season episode, 'The Larry Fay Story' (15/12/60), guest-starring Sam Levene as Fay and June Havoc as a rather subdued Texas Guinan type, involved itself in a completely different plot).

When, at the beginning of the 1960s, *The Untouchables* was enjoying such a television success, Warner Bros TV utilised a generous helping of Walsh's period footage (newsreel as well as the Warner film's 1939 footage) for its own racketeer-infested TV series, *The Roaring 20's* (in a rather anaemic imitation of *The Untouchables*).

During the 1940s (and into the 1950s) the gangster film, save for a few exceptions – such as *High Sierra* (WB, 1941), *The Big Shot* (WB, 1942), *Roger Touhy, Gangster* (20th-Fox, 1944), *Key Largo* (WB, 1948) and *White Heat* (WB, 1949) – gave way to the private detective phase which, as post-war French cineastes would observe, became generally known through its bleak outlook and dark ambience as film noir. The film noir's schizophrenic characters, intense atmosphere and psychological brooding (Fritz Lang's 1953 *The Big Heat* (Columbia) remains a good example) continued through to the latter part of the 1950s, by which time audiences had began to demand a more direct form of crime/underworld drama. An example of this changing direction (similar to the fantasy genre's evolution from 1940s gothic-horror creepings to 1950s science fiction's all-out alien monster invasions) was Don Siegel's hard-boiled, stylised (though virtually fact-free) account of the FBI's 1934 Public Enemy Number One *Baby Face Nelson* in 1957. Despite its rural 1930s country-boy-killer scenario, Siegel's film was to signal a nostalgic (and even more brutally violent) return to the Prohibition-era gangster – and the third major gangster film cycle, at the forefront of which were *The Untouchables* and *Al Capone*, with their gritty, violence-laden Prohibition gangster biographies.

Epilog Two: Themes and Genre Elements

For its storylines, *The Untouchables* drew upon various strands of criminal activity in US gangland history as background for their episodes, fusing these historical elements with the film genre's extrapolation of similar characters and events. Sources of inspiration for *Untouchables* scriptwriters came not only from the Prohibition-era mobsters and the Mid-West bandits of the Great Depression but also from gangster films of the 1930s and the 1950s. That the film genre, regardless of which type of characters were portrayed, followed certain basic story backgrounds is clearly evident in the series: namely, the violent milieu of bootlegging, gambling, political corruption, narcotics and kidnapping. These 'rackets' proved to be popular subjects of the urban American gangster film over two major cycles and multiple phases.

For obvious reasons, bootlegging and gambling were recurring themes in many films of the 1920s and early 1930s, followed intermittently by films which involved kidnapping and ransom as a lucrative business. Corrupt politics and business practices had been the subject of gangster films before the 1933 decline of Tammany[6] politics and was later exploited as the eroding element of a city or community in a phase of exposé films produced during the 1950s (*The Phenix City Story*, *Inside Detroit* and others) depicting citywide graft and civic corruption.

The depiction of the woman gangster, rather than the woman racketeer who was usually employed in the brothel-owning business (and not to be confused with the gangster's moll, either), did not arrive on the screen as a hard-boiled, gun-toting character until well after the mid-1930s demise of such Depression-era killers as Kate 'Ma' Barker and Bonnie Parker. Unfortunately, *The Untouchables* did not really pursue the killer-woman element in US gangster history (the male mobster's equivalent) as much as it enjoyed its own tough-minded, Texas Guinan-type women gangsters who were usually involved in the nightclub business.

For *The Untouchables*, the historical aspect (accuracy) always gave way to the genre element (action), a matter that would disgust students of history but would be quite happily accepted by viewers of early 1960s action-drama American television.

Bootleggers and bootlegging

'Bootlegging', the illegal traffic in liquor in violation of legislative restrictions on its manufacture, sale or transportation, became part of the American vocabulary during national Prohibition (1920–33). (Apparently, the word came from the early American practice of concealing flasks of illicit liquor in boot-tops during trade exchanges with the Indians.) In the colourful era of speakeasies and night-clubs, illegal liquor production and distribution led to the establishment of organised crime, which would persist long after the repeal of Prohibition.

The bootlegger flourished because the demand for alcohol reached an all-time high and various cunning, even spectacular, means of circumventing the law were employed. Smuggling across national borders was supplemented by fleets of foreign-registered rum-running ships, which operated outside territorial waters (the 12-mile limit). Rum-running (which actually included all manner of liquor) was a popular feature of many of the early gangster films. It also provided the greatest source of story inspiration for scriptwriters of *The Untouchables*, a rather obvious genre element since the series was intended to revolve around the exploits of Prohibition agents.

Among the early gangster films to employ bootlegging and its milieu as a story basis were *Twelve Miles Out* (MGM, 1927), where bootleggers John Gilbert and Ernest Torrence fight it out over the young Joan Crawford; *Burning Up Broadway* (Sterling Pictures, 1928), with revenue agents disguised as hijackers; *Ned McCobb's Daughter* (Pathé Exchange, 1929), in which Robert Armstrong runs his operation using trucks with false bottoms; and *Corsair* (UA/Art Cinema, 1931), where boot-legger Chester Morris shows that crime does indeed pay by successfully getting away with his financial rewards at the end.

The Untouchables enjoyed presenting various stories in which inventive and enterprising bootleggers attempted to keep the flow of booze going. 'The Matt Bass Scheme' (9/11/61), for instance, featured Telly Savalas as an ex-con who devises a 'foolproof' method for bringing bootleg alcohol to Frank Nitti in Chicago (he lays in a direct pipeline using Chicago's public waste-disposal facilities as a channel). Bootleggers were also seen to recruit a priest and a small community church for their operation to bring Canadian liquor into Chicago in the 'Canada Run' (4/1/62) episode. And refrigerated freight cars from the Boston fish market proved an ideal form of transportation for champagne in 'The Chess Game' (9/10/62). Ultimately, bootleggers took to bottling their own concoctions of spurious liquor.

After a decade of Prohibition, disregard of the law had become widespread, and in 1933 the 'noble experiment' was abandoned. In 'Takeover' (1/3/62), a third season story, father and son gangsters (Luther Adler and Robert Loggia) are seen battling for control of the Chicago beer market even on the eve of the repeal of the Eighteenth Amendment.

During the 1920s over seventy-five films were produced that featured bootleggers or used bootlegging as a cautionary element of the screenplay; the majority of them made a point of highlighting the evils of liquor consumption. One example, *Robes of Sin* (William Russell Prods, 1924) featured the attempts of a government agent to break up a gang of bootleggers while, unknown to him, his wife is associating with them. *Deliverance* (Stanley Advertising Co., 1928) followed a US senator as he conducted a survey of the effects of Prohibition before casting his vote on the Eighteenth Amendment (he voted in favour); while *Kid Gloves* (WB, 1929) saw fit to reverse the social trend by having Conrad Nagel's bootleg hijacker reformed by sympathetic socialite Lois Wilson. Since *The Untouchables* could not present a story that did not feature some sort of underworld villain, the series, while drawing on elements from these earlier films with a social view on the period, was forced to project the more exploitable gangster angle on the Prohibition era.

With the coming of sound in cinema (and now that the screaming tyres and chattering tommy-guns could be heard), the early 1930s roared with films featuring bootlegging (some eighteen films in 1931; sixteen in 1932; seventeen in 1933), before the phase finally fizzled out in the mid-1930s. *The Secret Six* (MGM, 1931), *The Public Enemy* (WB, 1931), the social melodrama *The Face on the Barroom Floor* (Criterion Pictures Corp., 1932), Victor Fleming's non-gangster film, *The Wet Parade* (MGM, 1932) and *Song of the Eagle* (Paramount, 1933), starring Charles Bickford as a bootlegger who, after Prohibition is finally repealed, goes directly into the protection racket, were among the more interesting (and relevant) releases during this period. These films, again, also served as inspiration for genre elements that surfaced in *The Untouchables*: the illicit stills, industrial alcohol, bootleg brandy and adulterated alcohol (in 'The Antidote' (9/3/61) a bootlegging ring even uses a process to reclaim industrial alcohol that has been denatured).

The Untouchables, with its franchise in Capone's Chicago, where the law was dry but the city was wet, presented more stories dealing with bootlegging than any other facet of gangland activity characteristic of that period of US history. While the series presented stories that concentrated at first on the careers of real-life Chicago, New York or Mid-West gangsters, bankrobbers and others, it soon turned to stories directly focusing on bootleggers. Only two bootleggger episodes were presented in the first season, followed by seven in the second season, nine in the third and eight in the last season. Of course, many more episodes involved bootlegging as a theme, but it was used merely as a backdrop for purposes of departing on a separate plotline.

With their bootlegging storylines set at various different dates throughout the 1920s (since the series was desperate for historical bases), the series was forced to leap backwards and forwards in Prohibition time to deliver relevant stories, ranging from the mid-1920s of 'The Genna Brothers' (during the third season) to the eve of repeal in 1933 (with 'The Waxey Gordon Story' (10/11/60) of the second season). Whatever the time period, the majority of these episodes, whether based on actual events or simply the scriptwriters' composites of historical events and characters, ultimately had to depend on the show of violence that characterised the struggle for power between rival gangs of bootleggers. As the producers were well aware, it became a feature that the series' audience expected (which in turn maintained or even increased viewer ratings).

Historically, what started out with the hijacking of other bootleggers' imported liquor soon evolved into a mainstream business with the establishing of the illegal brewery and the illicit still. The prevailing attitude of the general public during Prohibition that drinking was a minor violation, bordering on a lark, acted in Capone's favour. Stack's Ness is constantly flummoxed by the carefree attitude of the non-gangland types in the series who regularly offer him a drink or casually drink alcohol in his G-man presence. He seemed very much alone in pointing out to various police officials than an enormous industry had not gone out of existence with the Eighteenth Amendment but instead had been appropriated by racketeers and hoodlums. The Torrio–Capone mob, as it was known in the early days, hired the best brewmasters available (usually of German origin), even smuggling them into the US via Canada across Lake Michigan (as dramatised in 'The Monkey Wrench' (5/7/62) episode where Claude Akins, as a rival mobster, starts bumping them off on arrival!) and setting up their own chain of discreetly located breweries from which the beer was relayed to the consumer through an elaborately planned distribution system; Jack Klugman, in 'Eye for an Eye' (19/2/63), is busy organising hundreds of small merchants who retail whiskey supplied by him.

As something of a tableau that was more TV drama than actual history, *The Untouchables* has always been associated with the exciting, dramatic imagery of a Prohibition-era warehouse brewery being raided by Ness and his men in an explosion of action, as armour-plated trucks crash through huge doors, police spray the place with machine-gun bullets, axes chop into the sides of wooden brewery vats and foaming beer gushes across a body-strewn floor. This exciting footage, first created for the climax of part two of the *Desilu Playhouse* two-parter, was re-used over and over again in various episodes throughout the series' four seasons.

For television, the raiding of illicit stills and breweries by the Ness squad was always accompanied by a furious, violent gun battle, in which the mobsters, of course, sustain the heaviest body-count. Historically, it was quite a different story. When the real Eliot Ness and his men went to raid a brewery – and usually everyone knew about it in advance – the owners just left by the back door: they weren't going to shoot a federal man; it wasn't worth it. Also, to the real Ness, the brewing materials were often more important than the employees. Describing the outcome of one such raid in his 1957 book, Ness boasts:

> Only two men were on the premises, but it was worthwhile. We confiscated 62,000 gallons of wort [unfermented malt], 51 barrels ready for shipment, complete icing equipment, five 3,000-gallon pressure tanks, fifteen 3,000-gallon ageing tanks, special ventilating apparatus and a cooperage plant with 150 finished but empty barrels.[7]

For the series, a rather inventive ploy was devised in 'Cooker in the Sky', where guest gangster J. D. Cannon played a specialist imported from New York by the mob to construct a 'Ness-proof' plant, which he did for a while by locating the brewery in an upper floor of a factory.

Stories about the clever practice of using home stills turned up in two rather good episodes: 'Augie "The Banker" Ciamino' (9/2/61), where Keenan Wynn has his bootleg liquor made in hundreds of home stills by honest but frightened immigrants; and, similarly, 'The Genna Brothers' (2/11/61), as mentioned previously, in which Marc Lawrence and Antony Carbone organise alcohol cooking as a cottage industry throughout Chicago's Little Italy, conglomerating so many small home stills that they soon find themselves masters of a giant distilling enterprise.[8]

Industrial alcohol was the subject of 'The Antidote' (9/3/61), bootleg brandy the background to '90-Proof Dame' (8/6/61), champagne in 'The Chess Game' (9/10/62), the campus whiskey trade in 'The Snowball' (15/1/63), and in 'Eye for an Eye' (19/2/63) Klugman almost defeats the government's programme to stop the sale of liquor. Two other episodes also dealt with the extremely dangerous bay rum, known as 'the worst evil'. Michael Ansara and Alfred Ryder smuggled in the stuff in 'The Jamaica Ginger Story' (2/2/61), while Dane Clark's public health official tried to stop the flow in the 'Jake Dance' (21/1/63) episode. 'Thousands

Robert Stack's Ness in action, again.

drank this "canned heat",' observes Martin Short in his book of the Thames TV series *Crime Inc.* 'Others extracted it through a handkerchief. So many people were crippled for life by drinking adulterated Jamaica ginger that they formed a pressure group to get damages from the government.'[9]

Gambling and nightclubs
Colin McArthur's seminal study *Underworld USA* makes the following observation:

> Several commentators have pointed out that the puritan element in American life has

68

consistently caused legislation to be enacted against human desires and failings; hence the early and widespread legislation against gambling and prostitution – two of the first areas, together with strong-arm politics, to be taken over by racketeers and gangsters.[10]

Stories dealing with various forms of illicit gambling are scattered throughout *The Untouchables*. The numbers game, for instance, an illegal lottery popular among the low-income classes, was featured early on in the first season in 'You Can't Pick a Number' (24/12/59), where Ness is hot on the trail of the numbers racketeers following the knifing of a 'runner' (the collector who accepts the bets). While a similar set-up in 'The Troubleshooter' (12/10/61), revolving around the profitable punchboard game, described how the Chicago underworld imported a New York specialist in 'police contacts' (wonderfully played by Peter Falk with his quirky movie-gangster malevolence) in an effort to keep Ness from smashing the racket. Falk's bribery-with-violence specialist, having already been turned down by Ness, remains one of those rare *Untouchables* gangsters who manages to deliver a hefty slap to Ness's face and get away with it (at least for a short while)!

Much like his effect on the TV Chicago underworld in general, the television Ness was only able to dent organised crime's gambling operations. Whichever form of the betting game he investigated, Ness nabbed the minions with little or no problem, but usually failed to net the kingpins.

He took on bookmaking and the horse-racing wire service, respectively, in 'The Nick Acropolis Story' (1/6/61) and 'The Whitey Steele Story' (8/2/62). The former story, featuring a powerhouse performance from Lee Marvin as a granite-hard gangster (he even challenges the whole Nitti mob), reduced Ness and his squad to the role of interested observers while a three-way mob fight develops over the bookmaking game. The chilling conclusion to a doublecross subplot in this episode sees Marvin corner his treacherous henchman in a darkened flower shop and stalk him with a pair of enormous shears. In 'Whitey Steele', Ness rather ridiculously masquerades as the eponymous gangster of the title in an undercover ploy to amass evidence against the horse-racing wire-service operators who also happen to be peddling narcotics.

Slot-machines are the focus of 'One-Armed Bandits' (4/2/60), in which released prisoner Harry Guardino is blackmailed by gangsters into taking a job in their slot-machine organisation, while 'Man in the Middle' (5/4/62) features Martin Balsam as a wily slot-machine operator seeking personal revenge on the mob by setting up fellow gangster Gavin MacLeod's death (in a cunning move, Balsam puts extra tumbler weights in the machines MacLeod has hired from the mob to suggest profit-skimming); interestingly, Balsam also played a numbers boss in the 'Take a Number' episode of the contemporary gangland-set *Cain's Hundred* series around the same time. In the third season's 'The Contract' (31/5/62), Ness pursues hoodlum Frank Sutton, on the lam from the mob, to a gambling ship anchored off the California coast. Unfortunately, the episode doesn't make much of this interesting setting, which was exploited more fully in a 1959–60 series called *Mr Lucky* (based on the 1943 Cary Grant film by RKO).

The Untouchables inevitably linked gambling with the boom rackets of nightclubs, casinos and the more ambitious speakeasy venues, as well as the continuing profits to be made from prostitution. While feature films had cautiously suggested prostitutes and prostitution in the form of club 'hostesses', *The Untouchables* never really pointed up the world of prostitution in the Prohibition era (Capone, for instance, had been running Torrio's brothels since 1919) except for one especially harrowing episode, 'The White Slavers' (10/3/60). Larry James Gianakos regards 'White Slavers' as the series' finest episode, which, for its time it undoubtedly was; it also marked a peak in terms of the body-count. Gianakos describes the main gangster's comeuppance thus:

> The principal mafioso in this case is entrapped in the cellar of his hideaway by several of the women whose lives he has mutilated. The women approach closer and closer – as if to consume their captive – while his screams are muted by the gunplay going on on the floor above.'[11]

Nightclubs, like speakeasies, were the playgrounds of all things 'taboo' during Prohibition, where drinking, gambling and prostitution were rife. A characteristic feature of the gangster film iconography is the police raid on the nightclub, where masses of axe-wielding cops burst in through shattered doors and herd the panicked patrons away from the exits. While clubs in *The Untouchables* were never as lavish as Gladys George's hot spot in *The Roaring Twenties* (1939), the niteries of 'Ain't We Got Fun?' (12/11/59; in which Ted De Corsia's mob muscle in on the ownership of a club as a future outlet for his illicit whiskey), 'Jack "Legs" Diamond' (20/10/60), 'The Rusty Heller Story' (13/10/60), 'The Larry Fay Story' (15/12/60; depicting the famous El Fay nightspot of the late 1920s), 'The Silent Partner' (1/2/62; with Bert Convy playing a Joe E. Lewis type singer-comedian after Sinatra's compelling performance as the doomed entertainer in Charles Vidor's 1957 biography *The Joker Is Wild*), and other episodes delivered the music, smoke and chatter convincingly.

Jazz clubs, appropriately, turned up in 'Blues for a Gone Goose' (29/1/63; in which Kathy Nolan starred as the wife of a Chicago mobster who likes jazz music) and 'The Jazz Man' (30/4/63; a New Orleans-based story in which Ness impersonates a slain musician while on the trail of a narcotics supplier). Burlesque joints were the seedy end of the gangland establishments, as seen in the '90-Proof Dame' (8/6/61) episode where mobster owner (and bootlegger) Steve Cochran is described thus by Winchell's narration:

> Nate Kestor, former henchman of Capone. And still a very big noise with the mob. He maintained a pretence of legality by owning and running the Odeon Burlesque. [Then, over shots of a sultry stripper in action.] Kestor's shows were notoriously underdressed. His girls wore just enough to cover his real operation.

Politics and business

When Prohibition ended in December 1933, FBI head J. Edgar Hoover reckoned that gangsters, no longer able to peddle liquor, would turn to the kidnapping racket (following the impact of the 1932 Lindbergh case). But it didn't happen that way, at least not for the urban gangster. Instead, anonymous grey-flannel business suits inherited Capone's legacy of organised crime, and from it developed what became known as the Syndicate. These faceless figures, however, had always been there, higher up and remote from the general milieu, as Andrew Sarris reminds us: 'Most crime reporters were well aware that Capone could not have flourished as he did if the entire Chicago police force and municipal government had not been on the take.'[12]

Although the formation of the Eliot Ness Untouchables squad in 1929 was partly due to widespread corruption in the Chicago police department, the series (rather cautiously) presented only a few 'crooked' cops stories during its run; instead, they sought to depict other elements of the law enforcement service as corrupt or suggested that certain vigilante tactics were due to the burden of beaurocratic red tape. Federal prison officers in the two-parter 'The Big Train' (5 and 12/1/61) are seen to accept bribes to set up Capone's escape; Martin Balsam in 'Tunnel of Horrors' (26/10/61) is a former police officer turned crooked due to circumstances beyond his control; and Lee Marvin in 'A Fist of Five' (14/12/62) is a dedicated policeman who, frustrated by his inability to make arrests stick, forms a vigilante mob with his brothers. The depiction of the venal federal officers in 'The Big Train' caused an outcry, and Desilu subsequently shied away from any further 'reflections' of actual history; the characters played by Balsam and Marvin were portrayed as just a couple of well-meaning individuals who resented the restrictions placed on honest lawmen. (MGM's *The Secret Six*, in 1931, related to the story of a special police force, calling itself the 'Secret Six', which was comprised of six masked men representing the 'greatest force of law and order in the US'.[13])

The demise of the early 1930s gangster film cycle, it has been noted, was due not so much to the portrayal of the gangster-as-hero but more likely because these films also showed that certain elements of corruption in civic organisations and big-business corporations were linked to organised crime.

Chicago had been a 'wide-open town' since the mid-nineteenth century, run by saloon-owning gambler-politicians, until 1915, when William Hale ('Big Bill') Thompson, a Republican, was appointed mayor. Thompson subsequently delivered Chicago from the saloon-owning politicians to the biggest underworld power in Chicago crime, Johnny Torrio. After barely surviving an assassination attempt by Bugs Moran in January 1925, Torrio turned everything over to Capone, which included the mob's political connections, and then left Chicago. By 1926, Capone's turnover was put at $100 million a year, $30 million of which went on graft to police, judges and politicians.[14]

'Syndicate Sanctuary' (7/1/60), shown during *The Untouchables* first season, was the first story directly about political corruption, and related how an honest candidate for mayor is killed in a Chicago suburb. The southern area of Illinois known as 'Little Egypt' (11/2/60) became the title and setting (the fictitious town of Morraine) for a story in which undercover Agent Allison investigates the murder of an honest sheriff and a mayor.

When Democrat Anton Cermak took office following the defeat of Big Bill Thompson (by 667,529 to 475,613 votes), and started cleaning up Chicago, Frank Nitti and the Capone mob were furious; the two-parter 'The Unhired Assassin' (25/2 and 3/3/60) related a story that suggested Nitti had despatched a hit team to assassinate the crusading mayor.

In 'Testimony of Evil' (30/3/61) Ness tracks down a witness whose testimony can convict a gangster and influence an election. The always excellent Pat Hingle featured as an ambitious public figure who tries to take over the 1933 Chicago World's Fair, in a third-season story 'The Case against Eliot Ness' (10/5/62) (which was somewhat reminiscent of the takeover subplot in the earlier 'Unhired Assassin' episode). For 'Power Play' (19/10/61), Ness gives his full co-operation to the new head of a crime commission (played by the usually reassuring Wendell Corey, but now seen as a scheming brains-behind-it-all), only to discover that Corey actually runs an underworld syndicate.

The third-season episode 'The Silent Partner' (1/2/62) takes the political connection theme right to the top (the political power of finance) when Ness learns that the top brass of the Chicago underworld themselves have a boss (a boss of bosses?); in a clever gimmick, the anonymous character in the episode is glimpsed only in half-light and silhouette while issuing his instructions – remaining nameless to the end, in the closing credits he is simply billed as 'The Partner'. Winchell's introductory narration describes him thus:

> The most powerful man in the underworld and the least known. Only three top gangsters had ever met him. Only a handful of others knew he existed. A nameless, faceless somebody. Known only by rumour. Only as The Partner.

Perhaps as a footnote to gangland connections with politics, *The Untouchables* presented two episodes dealing, both directly and indirectly, with Nazis (albeit set a bit before their political time). In 'The Otto Frick Story' (22/12/60), German-American dope pedlars Jack Warden and Richard Jaeckel receive their supplies from charismatic Nazi Bund leader Francis Lederer in exchange for supporting Bund rallies. 'The Floyd Gibbons Story' (11/12/62), a back-door pilot for a period adventure series that failed to materialise, has Ness and the eponymous character of the title (Scott Brady) tackle the underworld outfit that is selling munitions metals to Nazi Germany. Both storylines are, of course, historically far-fetched, since they are set at the beginning of the 1930s; America and Germany were still both under the cloud of a depression, and the Bund didn't come into existence until the years immediately preceding US entry into the Second World War. Still, the stories did present a fascinating juxtaposition.

Unions and industry

Under Capone, the huge crime combination, still known today as the 'Outfit', took three evolutionary leaps to become the most sophisticated criminal organisation in America. Through violence and corruption he achieved the first by eliminating all his major competitors. His third great contribution to organised crime was to make the mob multi-ethnic. Jews, Irishmen, Germans, Poles: he did not discriminate. In many respects he was an equal opportunity employer.[15]

However, Capone's second evolutionary leap was into 'legitimate' business. In 1928 Cook County investigators found that ninety-one business associations and labour unions were controlled by racketeers, most of them in the Capone syndicate. They included the Food and Fruit Dealers, the Junk Dealers and Pedlars, the Candy Jobbers, the Newspaper Wagon Drivers, the Building Trade Council, the City Hall Clerks, the Glaziers, the Bakers, the Window Shade Manufacturers, the

Barbers, the Soda Pop Pedlars, the Ice-Cream Dealers, the Garbage Haulers, the Street Sweepers, the Banquet Organisers, the Clothing Workers, the Musicians, the Safe Movers, the Florists, the Motion Picture Operators, the Undertakers and the Jewish Chicken Dealers.[16]

This industrial racketeering included hiring out protection both to employers and unions ('The George "Bugs" Moran Story' (5/11/59); gaining control of the union to shake down industry ('The Frank Nitti Story'); and by extortion from 'vulnerable industries' (for example, 'The Artichoke King' (3/12/59), 'Hammerlock' (21/12/61) and 'Stranglehold' (4/5/61)) to avoid 'accidents' to their stock.[17]

The gangster films of the 1950s went on to explore (and dramatically exploit) many of these themes with *On the Waterfront* (Columbia, 1954; about the corruption-ridden dockworkers' union); *New Orleans Uncensored* (Columbia, 1954; also about dockworkers); *The Garment Jungle* (Columbia, 1957; featuring a union-breaking syndicate in the garment industry); *The Big Operator* (MGM, 1959; with Mickey Rooney as a Jimmy Hoffa-like corrupt labour boss) and others. *The Untouchables* featured a handful of plots that focused on the underworld's infiltration of, or their heavy-handed attempts to take over, various unions, trades and marketplaces. Besides 'The George "Bugs" Moran Story' (with its encroachment of a budding trucking union) and 'The Frank Nitti Story' (infiltration into the movie industry), discussed elsewhere (see p. 27), *The Untouchables* versions of price-fixing activities in the milk market (of all things) in 'The Larry Fay Story' (15/12/60) and the illegal use of facilities of the Boston fish transportation business in 'The Chess Game' (9/10/62) (the latter as a part of a bootlegging operation) were pretty much small fry when compared to three New York stories that approached extortion on a grand scale.

New York's enormous wholesale-produce market was the target of corruption in 'The Artichoke King', in which a restless-looking Jack Weston played notorious real-life mafioso Ciro Terranova, known as the Artichoke King because of his monopoly in this particular area of the market. The story tells of Terranova and partner Frankie Yale's attempt to take over the entire New York market area, before Ness (on 'special assignment') destroys their overly ambitious empire building. The historical background was of course correct, but the introduction of the TV Ness character into the proceedings was somewhat less than necessary in this case.

The other two New York-based episodes, 'Hammerlock' and 'Stranglehold', feature control of the baking industry and the Fulton fish market, respectively. These stories focused on the most notorious extortioners in the history of organised crime: Louis 'Lepke' Buchalter and Jacob 'Gurrah' Shapiro.[18] Although it was the New York special prosecutor's office of Tom Dewey that finally brought the two gangsters to justice in 1936, Ness was portrayed here as the one responsible for their downfall (in 'Hammerlock', an agent friend of Ness is killed by Buchalter's syndicate, which brings a vengeful Ness into the case; in 'Stranglehold', the authorities send for Ness and his squad to break the gang control).

In view of the Lepke/Gurrah syndicate's reputation for violence during the early 1930s, as Martin Short points out, they did not need to buy their way into any business. Lepke would tell the businessmen, 'You don't have to put us on your payroll; nothing will happen to you.' However, for the targeted businessmen, to hear such an assurance was the most frightening thing in the world. Although *The Untouchables*' versions made sure that plenty happened onscreen, the Lepke and Gurrah characters (as well as Dutch Schultz in these particular episodes) were presented more as boardroom businessmen who despatched their henchmen rather than involving themselves directly; it was these anonymous henchmen who ended up face down in the gutter after shooting it out with Ness's squad.

While any form of racketeering in *The Untouchables* always climaxed with a fearsome gun battle, such contemporary series as Lester Velie's *Target: The Corruptors* and Paul Monash's *Cain's Hundred*, spotlighting corruption in American cities, also focused on such themes as corrupt labour leaders ('The Organizer' and 'Prison Empire' episodes of *Target: The Corruptors*), dockworkers ('Dead Load') and control of the produce market ('Markdown on a Man') for *Cain's Hundred*. However, the racketeers' comeuppance in these series didn't usually result from a hail of lead, as *The Untouchables* would have it, but from a more restrained legal process. However, it is *The Untouchables*' form of television justice that is more likely to be remembered.

Women gangsters

The distaff side of the period gangster has always been represented by the notorious bank-robber gangs of Depression-era female icons Ma Barker and Bonnie Parker, the film versions of which usually play up the mythology of their violent careers rather than the actuality of their cheap banditry. This mythology developed from the highly publicised gunning-down of Bonnie Parker and Clyde Barrow in 1934 and Ma Barker in 1935, but it was a few years before thinly veiled film versions of their notorious careers were produced for the cinema. (There was, however, a feature-length documentary compilation released in 1936 called *The Vanishing Gangsters* (The Texas Roadshow Co., 1936) about the Department of Justice's 'sweeping drive to prosecute every lawbreaker' during the early 1930s which included footage and reference to both the Barker and Bonnie and Clyde cases, according to the AFI's *Catalog of Motion Pictures, 1931–1940*.[19])

Paramount's *Queen of the Mob* (Paramount, 1940) was perhaps the first Ma Barker film produced, with Blanche Yurka portraying the tough mobster chief in everything but name (she was called 'Ma' Webster and instead of being killed was captured by G-man Ralph Bellamy). Judith Anderson played a Ma Barker type in *Lady Scarface* (RKO, 1941), in which she heads a gang which commits a murder and robbery. But it wasn't until the 1950s that the actual character was named and directly represented on screen: by Jean Harvey in the 1952 *Gangbusters* TV series episode-compilation feature *Guns Don't Argue* (Visual Drama, 1955) and, later, by Lurene Tuttle as a particularly pathological Ma in the curious William J. Faris production, *Ma Barker's Killer Brood* (William J. Farris Prod., 1960); there was also a passing reference to the Barker character in Warner's *The FBI Story* (1959).

The second transmitted episode of *The Untouchables*, 'Ma Barker and Her Boys' (22/10/59), introduced one of the more interesting aspects of the series, with its presentation of women gangsters as main characters and serious Ness antagonists. Not that there were many stories dealing with the woman-as-gangster in the series, but the handful that were produced certainly made a lively change from the weekly shoot-outs involving the predominantly male mobsters.

Unlike the earlier gangster film cycles, where women were portrayed mainly as predators (the assorted molls and prostitutes), *The Untouchables* tended to present women, directly or indirectly connected with the underworld, merely as victims (the machine-gunned wife of the kidnap victim in 'The Purple Gang' (1/12/60), for instance). However, the seven or so stories that feature a strong female character stand out all the more for their powerful presentations of characters equally adept at outsmarting not only Ness and the law but also the more murderous gangland elements that were seen as duplicitous business partners or rival gangsters. Interestingly, it was Claire Trevor's Ma Barker, in 'Ma Baker and Her Boys', who came closest to what would eventually become the standard *Untouchables* male gangster: the blazing machine-gun, 'come and get me, copper!'-style hoodlum.

Trevor's Barker was, delightfully, equal parts Margaret Wycherly's Ma Jarrett (caring mom) and Cagney's Cody Jarrett (psychopathic killer) from *White Heat*. Her downfall, after a pitched battle with Ness and an army of police, is due not so much to the overwhelming power of law and order as to an internal family dispute (as son Fred and his new wife, played by a young Louise Fletcher, move out of the family group). Trevor's Ma Barker would be the series' only woman gangster to adopt the male gangster role of notoriety through direct violence. That the series got its knuckles rapped by the FBI for misrepresentation (whose case it originally was in the 1930s) may have been the reason why its next woman gangster story was a faint-hearted Bonnie and Clyde-type story (without actually being Bonnie Parker and Clyde Barrow, since that original case had nothing to do with Eliot Ness either).[20]

Anne Francis starred as the title character in 'The Doreen Maney Story' (31/3/60), where she and Christopher Dark, as her partner Sheik Humphries, played the leaders of a gang who rob armoured cars dubbed 'The Lovebirds'. Set in 1933, partly in the Depression-era belt of Tennessee, the story had Ness capturing Francis and setting a trap for her boyfriend when Ness estimates that he will try to ambush her escort to New York. While trying for a Depression-era Bonnie and Clyde effect (more blazing machine-guns, jaunty roadsters speeding along dusty country roads and such), the episode actually comes closer to the doomed couple of *They Live by Night* (RKO, 1948) than the ambitious and notoriety-loving duos of *The Bonnie Parker Story* (1958) or even the J. Edgar Hoover-influenced B-movie *Persons in Hiding* (1938; the first of a Paramount quartet of which *Queen of the Mob* was the fourth entry). Despite delivering quite a competent performance, Anne Francis does come across more as a lovesick hillbilly girl than the deadly female of, say, Peggy Cummins in *Gun Crazy* (U-I, 1950); however, this sexy, manipulative type would surface later in another mini-group of *Untouchables* woman gangster stories. The series' second-season opener, 'The Rusty Heller Story' (13/10/60), ushered in the sexy, clever, business-minded and manipulative woman gangster, this time symbolised by the 'sizzling, sensual' (*Daily Variety*, 14 October 1960) performance of Elizabeth Montgomery; similar performances were later delivered by Norma Crane in 'The Lily Dallas Story' (16/3/61) and Ruth Roman in 'Man Killer' (7/12/61).

While early films such as the 1932 *Madame Racketeer* (Paramount; with Alison Skipworth as a middle-aged larceny expert) and the 1937 *Federal Bullets* (Mono, 1937) (starring the granny-like Zeffie Tilbury as the guiding genius behind a crime ring) portrayed the old-lady-as-criminal-mastermind, *The Untouchables* equivalent was somewhat nearer to the more youthful advantages of Cummins's Annie Laurie Starr or even Susan Cabot's 'flirtatious floozie' in *Machine Gun Kelly* (1958).[21] These *Untouchables* gangland manipulators were able to match business smarts with the male gangsters to much better effect than if they had simply relied on the manipulative power of sex (the way Virginia Mayo drives Steve Cochran bug-eyed in *White Heat*). Montgomery's Southern-drawling Rusty Heller is perhaps the only one to use a *femme fatale* ploy, but then that is turned on Ness at nothing short of full throttle, marking the only instance in the series where Ness is in serious danger of actually falling for it. Meanwhile, however, Montgomery manages to manipulate two dangerous mob elements purely by her wits, in the end earning admiration even from that hard-as-a-rock authority figure Ness.

Both Norma Crane and Ruth Roman, in their respective episodes, manage to keep the male mobsters going through their paces without their once realising that this super-masculine underworld element is being commandeered by the intellect of a 'dame'. Crane uses her strength of character and intelligence to keep her gang from falling apart over the ransom following the kidnapping of a millionaire in 'The Lily Dallas Story'; and Roman is shrewd and forward-thinking enough to work her way into a partnership with the all-male Frank Nitti mob in 'Man Killer'.

June Havoc's Sally Kansas in 'The Larry Fay Story' (15/12/60), though supposedly the real-life Texas Guinan of New York's Roaring Twenties fame, is given a certain dignity as the duped girlfriend of speakeasy and nightclub owner Larry Fay. However, unfortunately, she ends up as just another mistreated moll who spills the beans to Ness in order to get even with her racketeer boyfriend. Havoc's character, rather sadly, descends into the category of the wronged woman whose idea of emotional revenge is simply selling out to Ness (as was the case with Joanna Barnes in '90-Proof Dame' (8/6/61) and Dolores Dorn in 'The Monkey Wrench' (5/7/62).

Perhaps the series' best performance of woman-as-thinking-gangster, next to Montgomery's Rusty Heller, is Patricia Neal's masterful speakeasy owner in 'The Maggie Storm Story' (29/3/62). Here, Neal's resourcefulness as a character caught between mobster elements as well as Ness (her speakeasy doubles as an auction room for illicit merchandise) produces an underworld businesswoman who doesn't much care what her business is and will not allow herself to be threatened from any quarter, whether it be gangster Vic Morrow's actual physical assault or Ness's probing investigation into the quantity of dope that goes under the hammer on the premises. Neal's Maggie Storm remains so spiritually undefeated throughout the story that you might think her character must be in some way related to that other great spiritually undefeated genre character, John Garfield's boxer Charlie Davis in Abraham Polonsky's 1947 *Body and Soul* (UA/Enterprise, 1947) (Garfield: 'What are you gonna do, kill me? Everybody dies.').

A final, unfortunate note on the distaff element in the series' scriptwriting department: of the fifty or so writers working on *The Untouchables*, only one woman screenwriter, it appears, was invited to compose a teleplay for the series – Kitty Buhler, with her assassination specialist story 'Come and Kill Me' (27/11/62) (in which Dan Dailey delivered a very assured performance as an instructor of novice hit men).

Narcotics

Dope, whether it be heroin, opium or any other substance, was the general term used in *The Untouchables* for all things narcotic and illicit. The stories dealing with narcotics were hardly any different from the bootlegging stories, except for the subject matter; more often than not they still involved importation and distribution, with just one or two intricate stories about the stealing of dope or its manufacture to slightly change tracks on the bootlegging theme. Unlike some contemporary US TV series, which often went down to street level to present bleak and uncomfortable stories about individual addicts and the consequences of addiction, such as *Cain's Hundred* (where Dorothy Dandridge's blues singer is trying to kick the habit in 'Blues for a Junkman', while vice baron David Brian attempts to get a young girl hooked in 'Degrees of Guilt') and *Target: The Corruptors* (in which addict Gena Rowlands gives birth to an addicted baby in 'The Poppy Vendor' episode), *The Untouchables* only depicted the importers and the larger-scale dealers and pedlars. Ness's target was the higher-ups in the narcotics business, though in the face of careful underworld organisation he rarely managed to nail them.

Nevertheless, the episodes that dealt with the importation of drugs presented their various action-filled gangland problems and hazards, though not always related historically to Ness and his squad. Steven Hill, for instance, brought about his own downfall by hijacking someone else's million-dollar shipment in 'Jack "Legs" Diamond' (20/10/60); while in 'Globe of Death' (5/2/63) Nitti and the mob conceal a $2 million shipment so cleverly that even though Ness knows the delivery (from the Far East) has been made he cannot locate the shipment to build a case for the government (the dope was secreted inside an enormous globe of the world!). Employing a change of setting, 'Murder under Glass' (23/3/61) and 'The Jazz Man' (30/4/63) move to New Orleans for their narcotics distribution stories. The former features an especially oily Luther Adler as an established dockside importer who ships his heroin in crates marked 'dry figs'; while the latter story uses the idea of a jazz musician's double-bass as a method of transporting the goods from New Orleans to Chicago.

The Untouchables writers made sure that the distribution of narcotics employed multiple offbeat forms and delivery methods. Jack Warden moved his dope while organising Nazi Bund rallies for his suppliers in 'The Otto Frick Story' (22/12/60). James MacArthur devises a method for selling narcotics and then gains possession of the merchandise by muscle in 'Death for Sale' (27/4/61). In a bold but completely insane move, syndicate narcotics dealer Harold J. Stone willingly gives Ness information on upcoming shipments but threatens to blow up an entire school while classes are in session if Ness attempts to do anything about it, in 'Pressure' (14/6/62). An interesting switch from the usual Ness-versus-narcotics dealer conflict appeared in the 'Junk Man' (26/2/63) episode, where Ness suddenly finds himself teamed up with Pat Hingle's undercover Federal Narcotics Bureau agent to thwart a giant scheme to distribute morphine across the whole of Chicago.

However, on his next narcotics assignment Ness takes something of a back seat during the investigation of an outbreak of systematic robberies of retail druggists, doctors' offices and wholesale drug houses, in 'A Seat on the Fence' (24/11/60), which guest-stars John McIntire as a crusty radio reporter who is threatened from both sides (Ness as well as the gangsters) when he refuses to divulge confidential information about the narcotics trade. Actually, the McIntire character's role is strangely not unlike the position Walter Winchell found himself in (as middle-man) when Lepke Buchalter turned himself in, via Winchell, to the FBI in 1939.

For 'Element of Danger' (22/3/62), Lee Marvin and Victor Jory are partners who control a formula for converting raw opium to heroin in vast quantities. During one pause in this enjoyably hectic story, Jory, in trying to introduce a note of reality to the zealous Ness, points out that 'The Sumerians had a dope problem three thousand years before the birth of Christ. As long as the opium poppy is grown anywhere in the world there'll be addicts.' Ness, of course, almost gives it a second's thought, only to continue his by-the-book objectives. Meanwhile, Marvin is on fine form as a particularly self-confident gangster (complete with straw skimmer propped at a rakish angle), fooling Ness about his real identity and motives for most of the story, and ending up, at the fiery climax, somewhat like the Cagney character in *White Heat*: Marvin goes crazy with a Thompson sub-machine-gun in the middle of a butane factory, spraying bullets in all directions until the inferno consumes him.

Kidnapping

Kidnapping, with the object of extorting large amounts of ransom money, became common in the US during the 1920s and 1930s. The kidnapping in 1932 of the infant son of the internationally known flyer Charles A. Lindbergh (a crime so hateful that Al Capone himself offered from his prison cell an unsolicited hand in cracking the case) spurred legislation imposing the death penalty for transporting a kidnapped victim across a state line. This incident, along with a few other highly publicised kidnappings (the 1933 abduction of millionaire oilman Charles F. Urschel by 'Machine Gun' Kelly, and the 1936 abductions of George Weyerhaeuser by Alvin Karpis and of Mrs Alice Stoll by Thomas H. Robinson Jr), started the film-makers' ball rolling, slowly and cautiously at first.

Kidnapping was, in the eyes of the Hays Office, a crime so distasteful that it had been banned from the screen since Paramount had released *Miss Fane's Baby Is Stolen* (in early 1934), before the interdiction had been enforced.[21] In this film, Baby LeRoy plays the child of a famous movie star who is kidnapped from his luxurious Beverly Hills home. This was the first kidnapping story to be produced following the famous Lindbergh case (except for the minor *The Important Witness* (State Rights/Tower Prods, 1933), in which a stenographer witnesses a gangland murder and is kidnapped by the killers). Even by the late 1930s the screenplay depiction of kidnapping was still a taboo area: *Held for Ransom* (International Film Corp./Grand National Film Inc., 1938), featuring a female federal agent who goes after the kidnappers of a wealthy man, was, according to information in the file on

(l. to r.) Robert Stack, Abel Fernandez, Nick Georgiade, Paul Picerni.

the film contained in the MPAA/PCA Collection at the AMPAS Library, refused a PCA certificate precisely because the ransom/kidnapping aspect of the picture, which was its main thrust, violated the Production Code.[22]

Inevitably, the subject of kidnapping featured in *The Untouchables* as a part of the series' trawl for exploitative stories generally (and rather loosely) relating to the period. However, only six or so episodes dealt with the subject as a crime that could conceivably involve Ness and his team, the majority of which appeared during the series' first season.

In 'The George "Bugs" Moran Story', Lloyd Nolan kidnaps the son of a union president (despite this, he is seen being particularly kind to the little lad). This is the only *Untouchables* plot to use a child as a kidnap victim as the crime was still

79

regarded as too unpalatable for audience tastes. 'The Tri-State Gang' (10/12/59) saw William Bendix kidnap bootlegging truck drivers before cold-bloodedly executing them; and 'The Vincent "Mad Dog" Coll Story' (19/11/59) even featured a subplot involving the kidnapping of a racehorse (which Clu Gulager's Coll planned later to shoot on a racetrack, *à la* Kubrick's *The Killing*).

A second-year episode, 'The Lily Dallas Story' (16/3/61), skirted around the kidnapping of a millionaire while actually presenting a thinly disguised version of the George 'Machine Gun' Kelly story (*The Untouchables* had learned from their experience with 'Ma Barker and Her Boys' (22/10/59) and the subsequent complaint by the FBI). However, all of these kidnap actions were peripheral to the episodes' main plots – which remained the capture or killing of an individual gangster by Ness. The two outstanding episodes to use kidnapping not only as a springboard for the action but also to revel in the seizure and detention of the hapless victims are the chilling 'The White Slavers' (10/3/60) (the abduction of young Mexican women for the purposes of prostitution, as discussed elsewhere (see p. 27)) and 'The Purple Gang'.

Turning up early in the series' second season, 'The Purple Gang' (1/12/60) provides the viewer with an excellent example of the basic elements and style of *The Untouchables*. The main storyline follows Detroit's Purple Gang and their attempts to kidnap a Capone-mob heroin courier, which in turn develops into a clash between Detroit and Chicago's underworld powers. The shipment of heroin in this case is simply there to present a supposedly logical (and legitimate) reason for involving the federal office of Ness and his squad, since at the time the story is set kidnapping was not yet a federal crime; and for such reasons Ness for the most part remains on the sidelines of the story, an observer of affairs that he does not at first fully comprehend. Actually, Ness is completely unaware of what is really going on until halfway through the story, by which time he has inadvertently allowed two murders to take place.

Following a string of mistaken-identity plot-points the episode winds up with another fierce gun battle, in which the Purple Gang's main mobster (played like a psychopathic Amboy Dukes street-gang leader by Steve Cochran) is chopped down by Ness. But, along the way to this inevitable showdown, Ness is also in pursuit of the Chicago mob courier (who turns out to be the wrong man); the Purple Gang kidnap the courier (still the wrong man), who is then killed and the right man is kidnapped by the gang (who turns out to be a Capone mob man); another of the mob's henchmen is held hostage for bargaining reasons; and Ness manages to grab the mob's ransom money on its way to the Purple Gang's payoff. Again, all that Ness and his squad really have to do here is to wait for the gangland factions to fight it out and then move in to arrest the survivors – a rather frequent (but nevertheless clever) Ness strategy in the series.

The return by the Purple Gang of the mob's heroin courier, Tornek (Werner Klemperer), remains, perhaps, one of the series' most cold-blooded sequences, and one that was singled out by contemporary critics. The courier's wife (Ilka Windish) receives a phone call, giving her the address of where she is to go with the ransom money, while Ness taps the phone line as a tracer. It is night as Mrs Tornek catches a cab to the given address, which is located in a bleak, run-down neighbourhood (her cab driver warns: 'This is no neighbourhood for a woman

Robert Stack's Ness dodging a hail of machine-gun bullets.

out alone.'). However, Ness's car has been following her. Alone on the street, the camera moves with her in medium shot as she walks down a dark alleyway (her footsteps resounding on the natural soundtrack). She stops and collects the gang's instructions ('Walk half block west and wait at mouth of alley.'). Continuing along the alleyway, slowly, carefully (like the nervous heroine of a Val Lewton picture), she is suddenly startled by the shriek of a baby crying out from one of the nearby buildings. Cut to – Mrs Tornek coming to the end of the alleyway, stepping out of the shadows into a gloomy half-light, then turning (in close shot) and reacting, via a sharp cut, to a shot of her husband hanging by his neck from a lamppost. Music hits sharply, mingling with her scream. Then, from an angle shot behind the hanging man, she runs towards the camera. Just as she reaches him, we cut to the rear window of a black car and a machine-gun as it starts blazing away. The woman's body is cut to the ground, and the gangsters' car speeds off. When Ness and Agent Hobson arrive on the scene, moments later, they find a note pinned to the hanging man's legs. In an insert, we see that it reads: 'Satisfied, Mr Ness?'

Darkly photographed by *Untouchables*' cinematographer Charles Straumer (with the gangland characters lit from low light which illuminates the face from unusual angles) and effectively cut (into a series of rapid shots) by film editor Ben Ray, this sequence, albeit for television, is as powerful in its delivery of a nasty-minded moment as anything in contemporary gangster films (the after-shock of the murder of the little girl in *Phenix City Story*, for instance). The prominent use of peculiar angles and enforced shadows was perfectly in keeping with the TV style of regular *Untouchables* director Walter Grauman.

Epilog Three: ABC TV and Television Violence

In 1954 the US Senate assumed primary responsibility for scrutiny of television content. The examination of television's effects on the younger elements of the audience came under what eventually developed into a ten-year Senate study of juvenile delinquency. The initial hearings on television were held in June and October 1954 under the chairmanship of Senator Robert C. Hendrickson. Senator Kefauver interpreted part of the subcommittee's mandate as to determine 'what the long-range effects of television may be on the Nation's youth'. As a result of these mid-1950s hearings, the industry allowed its knuckles to be rapped but suffered no significant changes to its operation.[24]

While the 1954 Hendrickson–Kefauver investigation was prompted by the fear that television was a contributory factor to the growing crime rate, the 1961 probe came about because Senator Thomas J. Dodd of Connecticut (Democrat) reacted to what he felt was the TV industry's unacceptable use of violence to spice up their programmes (in order to boost ratings and therefore increase revenues).

*

Both the ABC TV network and *The Untouchables* reached their respective peaks in 1960. It was noted by the industry that *The Untouchables* was probably the most violent series on television at that time, which, rather alarmingly, appeared to account for its popularity. And it was this ratings success that delivered the ABC TV network to top position among the then three US TV networks (the others being established industry giants NBC and CBS). Until this time, ABC had always been regarded as 'the also-ran network'.

In 1953, the network merged with United Paramount Theaters and, with the heavy infusion of capital provided by the merger, began developing programmes in earnest.[25] It also made the clever move of approaching film studios for products, which resulted in the landmark deal of 1954 that brought the Walt Disney studio into television. Their popular *Disneyland* anthology became ABC's first major hit series. Then, in 1955, an arrangement with Warner Bros produced another hit series, *Cheyenne*, and marked that studio's first venture into television.[26]

Although ABC started winning the ratings battle, it was soon apparent that all their prize programmes had a violent content (the Westerns *Wyatt Earp*, *Colt .45*, *Lawman*, and later the private-eye series *77 Sunset Strip*, *Bourbon Street Beat*, *Hawaiian Eye*). Since hitting their peak with *Cheyenne*, ABC became identified with the 'action-adventure' series, and for a brief period during the 1960–61 season, the network led the primetime ratings war. ABC's revenues increased at a rate that seemed to equal the combined gains of both its network competitors. But then, in the spring of 1961, CBS regained its edge.[27]

*

By the late 1950s, all three networks had moved into telefilm production with a broad sweep. Violent action series became the principal weapons in their ratings war. Mirroring the strong Warner Bros–ABC programme production tie, the telefilm producer MCA (the TV subsidiary of Universal Pictures) formed a strong association with NBC.[28]

The number of Westerns and police/detective dramas increased enormously, while their standards declined rapidly. Sensing a lack of originality in their product, producers compensated by lacing their episodes with sex and violence, but by the spring of 1961 American viewers were objecting to this cheap strategy more vocally than before.[29] Pressure groups were being formed, with the Italian-Americans, in particular, bearing down on *The Untouchables* by boycotting the products advertised on the series.

The crunch finally came in May 1961 when President Kennedy's newly appointed FCC commissioner Newton N. Minow addressed the annual gathering of the National Association of Broadcasters in the nation's capitol. Minow shocked his audience by characterising US television as a 'vast wasteland', which he defined as

> a procession of game shows, violence, audience participation shows, formula comedies about totally unbelievable families, blood and thunder, mayhem, violence, sadism, murder, Western bad men, private eyes, gangsters, more violence, and cartoons, and endlessly, commercials, many screaming, cajoling and offending. And most of all, boredom.[30]

As television historian William Boddy observes, Minow's phrase – 'vast wasteland' – crystalised the accumulated public and critical disenchantment with commercial television and immediately entered the vocabulary of public debate.[31]

While sponsors shied away from any hint of responsibility and network chiefs denied that they had encouraged the studios to inject gratuitous violence into their programmes, Dorothy Brown (Continuity Acceptance Editor) of ABC was quoted in *TV Guide* magazine (27 May 1961) as promising a new look for the 1961–62 season: 'We will have a balanced and lighter programme schedule next season, which makes for a less violent picture overall. . . . There will be considerably less violence [but] sex is here to stay.'

In June 1961, Senator Dodd, as chairman of the Senate Subcommittee on Juvenile Delinquency, opened what became nearly three years of intermittent hearings in which he set out to prove that there was a direct cause-and-effect relationship between television violence and violent behaviour in the population (in particular, children), alongside open criticism of the media for failing to self-regulate and curb violence on the air. In June and July of 1961, and again in 1964, his hearings produced evidence that network officials continually ordered TV programmers and film studios to increase the violent content in programmes for the sake of ratings.[32]

Prior to the launch of the 1961–62 season, with the networks holding their breath on whether ABC or NBC would move ahead or CBS would retain its national Nielsen ratings leadership, the game of competitive slotting saw NBC pit their middle-of-the-road musical variety show *Sing Along with Mitch* (featuring record producer-arranger Mitch Miller) against 'the "pappy" of the high-rated violence shows', *The Untouchables*, in the Thursday night 10 to 11 slot. 'It's a toughie for Mitch Miller,' observed *Variety* (20 September 1961), 'but if the public goes for his hour showcase, it could portend the beginning of the end for the no-holds-barred violence sagas.' *Sing Along with Mitch*, surprisingly, tuned its way up to number sixteen programme position, while *The Untouchables* took a one-way ride back to number forty-one.

On the FCC edict to 'clean up' violence, Robert Stack declared to *Variety* (4 October 1961) that

> they talk in generalizations. Of course the public wants less violence in its television diet, but until the networks, the ad agencies and the Federal agencies can agree on a yardstick – when it crosses the line between dramatic action necessary to the storyline – and becomes violence for violence sake, the material shown on television will remain the same. Only exception is that there will be a few very dull shows and a few violent ones because of network and ad agency pressures.

It *was* the beginning of the end, at least for a short while.

In 1968, the National Commission on the Causes and Prevention of Violence held hearings on the role of the mass media. In 1969, the surgeon general's joint Inquiry on Violence with the National Institute of Mental Health attempted to establish what harmful effects, if any, televised crime, violence and antisocial behaviour have on children. And in 1972, shortly after publication of the surgeon general's report, the Senator John Pastore hearings – in which all twelve members of the 1969 committee were questioned – came to its inconclusive conclusion that television violence can affect some of the viewers some of the time.[33]

Notes

1. The 36.1 rating, as measured by the A. C. Nielsen Company, means that on the average, 36.1 per cent of all TV homes in America tuned in to this programme during its transmission in April 1959.
2. Andrew Sarris, 'Big Funerals: The Hollywood Gangster, 1927–1933', *Film Comment*, May–June 1977, p. 6.
3. Carlos Clarens, 'Hooverville West: The Hollywood G-Man, 1934–1945', *Film Comment*, May–June 1977, p. 12.
4. The Production Code, a self-regulatory code of ethics created in 1930 by the Motion Picture Producers and Distributors of America (MPPDA), under Will H. Hays, and put into effect in July 1934, with Joseph I. Breen as director, all but outlawed the gangster film. With all the potential profits to be made from the popular gangster genre, the Hollywood producers needed a loophole. Hollywood's gamble was that if it supplied a new series of gangster films that focused on heroic cops, the law enforcement profession's enthusiasm would overwhelm any outside protests. The obvious candidate for this idealised cop would be J. Edgar Hoover's G-man. The producers requested, and were granted, an exemption from the Code's anti-gangster rules, and the G-man films of 1935 that established the public image of Hoover's FBI were the direct result of this temporary exemption from the Production Code (Richard Gid Powers, *G-Men:*

Hoover's FBI in American Popular Culture [Illinois: Southern Illinois University Press, 1983], pp. 68–73).

5. The colourful underworld character Larry Fay, along with his protégé Texas Guinan (famous nightclub entertainer and a former actress who had starred in several Western films as a sort of feminine W. S. Hart between 1917 and 1929), ruled Broadway's nightlife up until his death in 1930; he was shot by a disgruntled employee in one of his own nightclubs. Guinan operated the Fay-backed El Fay and Del Fay clubs as well as the popular nightclubs that bore her own name. She died in 1933 following an intestinal operation in Vancouver, BC.

6. Tammany Hall was the popular name of the executive committee of the Democratic Party in New York City historically exercising political control. The society's appeal to particular ethnic and religious minorities and the bribing of rival political faction leaders made the name Tammany Hall synonymous with urban political corruption.

7. Eliot Ness and Oscar Fraley, *The Untouchables* (London: Pan Books, 1960), p. 69.

8. Robert J. Schoenberg, *Mr Capone* (London: Robson Books, 1992), p. 82.

9. Martin Short, *Crime Inc.* (London: Thames Methuen, 1984) p. 73.

10. Colin McArthur, *Underworld USA* (London: Secker and Warburg/BFI, 1972), p. 60.

11. Larry James Gianakos, *Television Drama Series Programming: 1959–1975* (Metuchen, NJ: The Scarecrow Press, 1978), p. 262.

12. Sarris, 'Big Funerals', p. 7.

13. Historically, 'The Secret Six' (under the chairmanship of businessman Robert Isham Randolph) were known more formally as the Citizens' Committee for the Prevention and Punishment of Crime, a special committee of the Chicago Association of Commerce which was made up of a hundred Chicago lawyers, bankers and businessmen, with its own staff of investigators, statisticians and clerks. They were known as 'The Secret Six' to maintain a closely guarded anonymity to ensure their continued wellbeing. The 'Six' forced prosecutors to bring cases against protected gangsters and persuaded the Justice Department to send Eliot Ness to Chicago to harass the Capone organisation. Its most famous contribution to law enforcement lore was the Public Enemies List, which had started in April 1923, with Al Capone heading the list (Powers, *G-Men*, p. 23).

14. Short, *Crime Inc.*, pp. 60–67.

15. *Ibid.*, p. 92.

16. *Ibid.*, p. 91.

17. McArthur, *Underworld USA*, p. 61.

18. Short, *Crime Inc.*, p. 280.

19. *The American Film Institute Catalog of Motion Pictures Produced in the United States F3. Feature films, 1931–1940* (Berkeley: University of California Press, 1993).

20. Ida Lupino played a character called Ma Gantry in Quinn Martin's 1974–75 series *The Manhunter* ('The Ma Gantry Gang' episode), in which she and her sons rob trains during the Depression-era days.

21. David Will, '3 Gangster Films: An Introduction', in David Will and Paul Willemen (eds), *Roger Corman* (Edinburgh Film Festival, 1970), p. 72.

22. Clarens, 'Hooverville West', p. 12.

23. *The American Film Institute Catalog of Motion Pictures.*

24. Willard D. Rowland Jr, *The Politics of TV Violence: Policy Uses of Communication Research* (Beverly Hills, CA: Sage, 1983), pp. 101–4.

25. Les Brown, *The New York Times Encyclopedia of Television* (New York: Times Books, 1977), p. 2.

26. Tim Brooks and Early Marsh, *The Complete Directory to Prime Time Network TV Shows* (New York: Ballantine Books, 1979), p. xv.

27. Ed Papazian, *Medium Rare: The Evolution, Workings and Impact of Commercial Television* (New York: Media Dynamics, 1989), pp. 38–39.

28. William Boddy, *Fifties Television: The Industry and Its Critics* (Chicago, IL: University of Illinois Press, 1990), p. 238.

29. Papazian, *Medium Rare*, p. 39.
30. *Ibid.*, pp. 39–40.
31. Boddy, *Fifties Television*, p. 226.
32. Brown, *Encyclopedia of Television*, p. 158.
33. *Ibid.*, p. 596.

PART THREE

Robert Stack in characteristically humourless mood.

Episode Guide: *The Untouchables* (ABC TV, 1959–63)

After the credits/cast for the original two-part presentation, the episode guide follows its seasons of original transmission (generally running from October to April). The list of the series' regular cast indicates the seasons in which the performers appeared (if this constituted less than the entire production). Each of the series' four seasons is preceded by the relevant technical credits. The individual episodes (numbered merely to indicate order of transmission) cite the title, followed by the date of first US transmission; script credit, director credit and main guest performers; and a brief plot outline.

Key to Abbreviations

Prod: Producer; *Exec prod*: Executive producer; *Assoc prod*: Associate producer; *Prod super*: Production supervisor; *d*: Director; *sc*: Script; *Ph*: Photography; *Art dir*: Art director; *Set decor*: Set decorator; *Film ed*: Film editor; *Mus*: Music; *Choreog*: Choreography; *Asst dir*: Assistant director; *Ph effects*: Photographic effects; *Prop master*: Property master; *Cost*: Costumes, Costumer; *Sound eng*: Sound engineer; *Nar*: Narration, Narrator.

'The Untouchables'

Westinghouse–Desilu Playhouse: 'The Untouchables', parts one and two (NBC TV, tx 20 and 27/4/59).

> *Prod* Quinn Martin; *Exec prod* Bert Granet; *Assoc prod* Jack Aldworth; *Dir* Phil Karlson; *Sc* Paul Monash, based on the book *The Untouchables* (New York, 1957) by Eliot Ness and Oscar Fraley; *Ph* Charles Straumer; *Art dir* Ralph Berger, Frank T. Smith; *Set decor* Sandy Grace; *Film ed* Robert L. Swanson; *Mus* Wilbur Hatch; *Choreog* Jack Baker; *Sound* Cam McCulloch; *Asst dir* Vincent McEveety; *In Charge of Prod* Desi Arnaz; *Cost* Jerry Bos, Maria Donovan; *Makeup* Ed Butterworth; *Hairstyles* Lorraine Roberson.

CAST: Robert Stack (Eliot Ness), Keenan Wynn (Joe Fuselli), Barbara Nichols (Brandy La France), Patricia Crowley (Betty Anderson), Neville Brand (Al Capone), Bill Williams (Martin Flaherty), Joe Mantell (George Ritchie), Bruce Gordon (Frank Nitti), Peter Leeds (Lamarr Kane), Eddie Firestone (Eric Hansen), Robert Osterloh (Tom Kopka), Paul Dubov (Jack Rossman), Abel Fernandez (William Youngfellow), Paul Picerni (Tony Liguri), John Beradino (Johnny

Giannini), Wolfe Barzell (Picco), Frank Wilcox (Beecher Asbury), Peter Mamakos (Bomber Belcastro), Wally Cassell (Phil D'Andrea), Herman Rudin (Mops Volpe), Richard Benedict (Furs Sammons), Bern Hoffman (Jake Guzik), Frank De Kova (Jimmy Napoli), James Westerfield (Ed Marriatt); narrated by Walter Winchell.

Desilu Productions; black and white; 105 min. (also transmitted as 98 min).

The Series

REGULAR CAST: Robert Stack (Eliot Ness), Anthony George (Agent Cam Allison; first season only), Nicholas Georgiade (Agent Enrico Rossi), Jerry Paris (Agent Martin Flaherty), Steve London (Agent Jack Rossman), Paul Picerni (Agent Lee Hobson; from second season), Abel Fernandez (Agent William Youngfellow; from second season); Bruce Gordon (Frank 'The Enforcer' Nitti), Frank Wilcox (Beecher Asbury).

Season One

Exec prod Quinn Martin; *Prod* Charles Russell, Norman Retchin, Sidney Marshall, Paul Harrison, Josef Shaftel, Roger Kay, David Heilweil; *Asst to exec prod* Arthur Fellows; *Prod super* W. Argyle Nelson; *Prod manager* Lloyd Richards; *Asst dir* Vincent McEveety, Sergei Petschnikoff, Marvin Stuart, John E. Burch; *Casting* Kerwin Coughlin; *Story/script ed* Harry Fried; *Ph* Charles Straumer, Robert B. Hauser; *Ph effects* Howard A. Anderson Co.; *Editorial super* Bill Heath; *Film ed* Robert L. Swanson, Ben H. Ray, Richard Fritch, George J. Nicholson, Jack Foley, Edward Biery, Floyd Knudtson; *Art dir* Ralph Berger, Frank T. Smith, Rolland M. Brooks; *Set decor* Sandy Grace, Ross J. Dowd, Frank Wade; *Prop master* Charles West, Irving Fineberg (Feinberg), Donald Smith, Albert M. Joyce, Allan Levine, Jack Briggs; *Cost* Frank Delmar, Byron Munson; *Makeup* Jack Young, Kiva Hoffman, Gus Norin; *Hair stylist* Irene Beshon *Mus theme composed by* Nelson Riddle; *Lyrics* Sidney Miller (episode five only); *Mus super* Ted Roberts; *Sound* Glen Glenn Sound Co.; *Sound eng* Cam McCulloch, Karl Zint (Karl E. Zint), T. T. Triplett, Frank McWhorter, Harry Smith; *Sound ed* Josef von Stroheim, Joseph G. Sorokin; *Nar* Walter Winchell.

A Desilu production in association with Langford Productions.

1. 'The Empty Chair' (15/10/59)

sc David Karp, story by Ernest Kinoy *d* John Peyser
CAST: Nehemiah Persoff (as Jake 'Greasy Thumb' Guzik), Barbara Nichols, Betty Garde, Wally Carroll, Herman Rudin.

Ness uses Guzik's niece as the key to cracking the mob, leadership of which is now disputed by Guzik and Nitti.

2. 'Ma Barker and Her Boys'
(22/10/59)

sc Jeremy Ross *d* Joe Parker

CAST: Claire Trevor (as Ma Barker), Adam Williams, Louise Fletcher, Joe DiReda, Peter Baldwin, Vaughn Taylor.

Ness and his team pursue the middle-aged Ma Barker and her two sons to a small Florida resort.

3. 'The Jake Lingle Killing' (29/10/59)

sc Robert C. Dennis and Saul Levitt, story by Levitt *d* Tay Garnett
CAST: Jack Lord, Charles McGraw, Herb Vigran (as Jake Lingle), Philip Pine.

When a Chicago news reporter is

murdered, Ness forms an alliance with a private detective to move against a bootlegging outfit.

4. 'The George "Bugs" Moran Story' (5/11/59)

sc David Karp *d* Joe Parker
CAST: Lloyd Nolan (as Bugs Moran), Jack Warden, Chuck Hicks, Harry Shannon, Peter Baldwin, Robin Warga.

Notorious gangster Bugs Moran moves to take over a growing trucking union by kidnapping the small son of its president.

5. 'Ain't We Got Fun?' (12/11/59)

sc Abram S. Ginnes *d* Roger Kay
CAST: Cameron Mitchell, Ted De Corsia, Phyllis Coates, Timothy Carey, Joseph Buloff.

With Prohibition doomed by 1933, Chicago's gangsters turn to other sources for income and begin to muscle into nightclubs and restaurants.

6. 'The Vincent "Mad Dog" Coll Story' (19/11/59)

sc Charles Marion *d* Andrew McCullough
CAST: Lawrence Dobkin (as Dutch Schultz), Clu Gulager (as Mad Dog Coll), Susan Storr.

Ness moves in to collar Dutch Schultz for income tax evasion and Coll for kidnapping.

7. 'Mexican Stakeout' (26/11/59)

sc Alvin Sapinsley and Robert C. Dennis, story by Sapinsley *d* Tay Garnett
CAST: Vince Edwards, Joe Ruskin, Byron Foulger, Stafford Repp, David Renard.

Frustrated when a case he has been preparing for two years falls apart because of the disappearance of a key witness, Ness and an aide pursue a trail which leads to Mexico.

8. 'The Artichoke King' (3/12/59)

sc Harry Essex *d* Roger Kay
CAST: Jack Weston, Bob Ellenstein, Al Ruscio, Mike Mazurki.

Ness and his federal squad move in to clean up gangster influence in New York's wholesale produce market.

9. 'Tri-State Gang' (10/12/59)

sc Joseph Petracca *d* Allen H. Miner
CAST: William Bendix, John Ward, Roxanne Berard, Alan Hale Jr, Gavin McLeod, Jay Adler.

Ness is on the trail of Leganza (Bendix), a hijacker and kidnapper.

10. 'The Dutch Schultz Story' (17/12/59)

sc Jerome Ross and Robert C. Dennis, story by Ross *d* Jerry Hopper
CAST: Lawrence Dobkin (as Dutch Schultz), Mort Mills, Robert Carricart, Maggie Mahoney, Richard Reeves.

Ness and his squad nail Dutch Schultz on a tax case and Ness refuses a large cash offer to return the evidence.

11. 'You Can't Pick a Number' (24/12/59)

sc Henry Green *d* Richard Whorf
CAST: Darryl Hickman, Jay C. Flippen, Chris White, Doreen Lang, George Ramsey, Harry Tyler, Whit Bissell, King Calder.

In an all-out drive to crush the flourishing numbers racket in 1932 Chicago, Ness concentrates on the First Ward where the knifing of a collector may provide a lead.

12. 'Underground Railway' (31/12/59)

sc Leonard Kantor d Walter E. Grauman
CAST: Cliff Robertson, Virginia Vincent, Joe DeSantis, Murray Roman, Bob Hopkins.

Ness is in pursuit of a notorious crook who undergoes plastic surgery to emerge as handsome after unusual ugliness.

13. 'Syndicate Sanctuary' (7/1/60)

sc George F. Slavin prod/d Paul Harrison
CAST: Gail Kobe, Anthony Caruso, Jack Elam, Douglas Dumbrille, Frank Wolf.

When an honest candidate for mayor is killed in a Chicago suburb, Ness uncovers a far-reaching plot by the mob.

14. 'The Noise of Death' (14/1/60)

sc Ben Maddow d Walter E. Grauman
CAST: J. Carrol Naish, Rita Lynn, Mike Kellin, Henry Silva, Charlie Hicks, Karen Docker, Joi Lansing.

Ness observes as a district Mafia boss and his top protection racket collector battle it out for position in the crime society.

15. 'Star Witness' (21/1/60)

sc Charles O'Neal d Tay Garnett
CAST: Jim Backus, Marc Lawrence, Dorothy Morris, Jay Warren, Sal Armetta.

Ness takes advantage of internal strife in the mob to convict a top hoodlum.

16. 'The St. Louis Story' (28/1/60)

sc Joseph Petracca d Howard W. Koch
CAST: David Brian, Leo Gordon, Richard Bakalyan, Tom Trout, Bernard Fine, Lillian Bronson, Rita Duncan, Percy Helton.

Ness and his federal agents enter the scene when a St Louis gang robs a US mail truck.

17. 'One-Armed Bandit' (4/2/60)

sc E. Jack Neuman d Walter Grauman
CAST: Harry Guardino, Larry Gates, John Beradino.

Released prisoner Frank O'Dean (Guardino) is blackmailed by slot-machine gangsters into taking a job in their organisation.

18. 'Little Egypt' (11/2/60)

sc Joseph Petracca d John Peyser
CAST: Fred Clark, John Marley, Norman Alden, Susan Cummings, Jimmy McCallion, Sam Gilman.

Ness assigns Agent Allison to work undercover when an honest sheriff and a mayor are murdered.

19. 'The Big Squeeze' (18/2/60)

sc W. R. Burnett and Robert C. Dennis, story by Burnett prod/d Roger Kay
CAST: Dan O'Herlihy, Dody Heath, John Hoyt, Bill Forrester.

Ness works to trap leading bank robber Ace Banner (O'Herlihy) into an error which would uncover the evidence necessary to arrest him.

20 and 21. 'The Unhired Assassin' [parts one and two] (25/2 and 3/3/60)

sc William Spier d Howard W. Koch
CAST: Robert Middleton (as Mayor Anton Cermak), Joe Mantell (Giuseppe Zangara), Lee Van Cleef, Claude Akins, Richard Deacon, Frank De Kova, Robert Gist.

The stories relate an attempt by members of imprisoned Al Capone's mob to take over the 1933 Chicago World's Fair by eliminating crusading Mayor Cermak. (Re-edited for feature release as Guns of Zangara.)

22. 'The White Slavers' (10/3/60)

sc Leonard Kantor d Walter Grauman
CAST: Betty Field, Mike Kellin, Dick York, Theona Bryant, Mona Knox, Jim Anderson.

When racketeer operations shift to Mexico, Ness seals off the border and, with the co-operation of a reformed ally of the operation, stages a raid to end the activities of the mob.

23. 'Three Thousand Suspects' (24/3/60)

sc Robert C. Dennis d John Peyser
CAST: Leslie Nielsen, Peter Leeds, Benny Burt, James Flavin, Francis De Sales, Howie Storn.

When a prisoner is killed in jail for threatening to 'sing' to the police, Ness has Tom Sebring (Nielsen), another prisoner, act as an informer.

24. 'The Doreen Maney Story' (31/3/60)

sc Jerome Ross d Robert Florey
CAST: Anne Francis, Christopher Dark, Connie Hines, George Mitchell.

Ness finds that the trail to a gang robbing armoured trucks leads to a man and woman known as 'The Lovebirds'.

25. 'Portrait of a Thief' (7/4/60)

sc Herbert Abbott Spiro d Walter Grauman
CAST: Edward Andrews, Henry Jones, Charles McGraw (as Johnny Torrio).

Ness, moving in to halt the flow of alcohol to bootleggers, uncovers a scandal in a respected drug firm.

26. 'The Underworld Bank' (14/4/60)

sc Aben Kandel d Stuart Rosenberg
CAST: Thomas Mitchell, Peter Falk, Virginia Vincent, Ernest Sarracino, Penny Santon, Bernard Kates, Val Avery.

Ness tangles with a crooked financial genius who has organised a 'package deal' for crime operations (aka 'Underground Bank').

27. 'Head of Fire, Feet of Clay' (21/4/60)

sc Ben Maddow d Walter Grauman
CAST: Jack Warden, Madelyn Rhue, Nehemiah Persoff, Patsy Kelly, Virginia Christine, Leon Gordon.

Ness finds himself in a strange situation when an old school pal, now allied with the rackets, uses him as bail in a blackmail plot (aka 'Bullets from Heaven').

28. 'The Frank Nitti Story' (28/4/60)

sc Lee Blair Scott, story by Harry Essex d Howard W. Koch
CAST: Bruce Gordon (as Frank Nitti), Myron McCormick, Dick Foran, Frank Albertson, Phyllis Coates.

Ness moves in to break up Nitti's extortion operations against the movie industry.

Season Two

Exec prod Jerry Thorpe; Prod Josef Shaftel, Walter E. Grauman, Lloyd Richards, Alan Armer; Assoc prod Lloyd Richards; Prod super W. Argyle Nelson; Prod manager Marvin Stuart; Asst dir Vincent McEveety, Russ Haverick, Ed Killy, Sergei Petschnikoff, Jay Sandrich; Casting Stalmaster-Lister Co.; Story/script ed Harry Fried; Ph Charles Straumer; Ph effects Howard A. Anderson Co.; Editorial super Bill Heath; Film ed John Foley, Elmo Veron, Ben H. Ray, Robert Fritch, William B. Murphy, Ed Sampson; Art dir Ralph Berger, Frank T. Smith, Rolland M. Brooks, Bill Glasgow, Howard Hollander; Set decor Sandy Grace; Prop master Irving Feinberg, Allan Levine; Cost Frank Delmar; Makeup Kiva Hoffman; Hair stylist Irene Beshon, Anna Malin, Annabel, Beth Langston; Mus Nelson Riddle; Mus super Robert Raff; Sound Glen Glenn Sound Co.; Sound eng T. T. Triplett; Sound ed Joseph G. Sorokin, John H. Post, Wayne Fury, Ross Taylor; Nar Walter Winchell.

A Desilu production in association with Langford Productions.

29. 'The Rusty Heller Story' (13/10/60)

sc Leonard Kantor *d* Walter Grauman
CAST: Elizabeth Montgomery, Harold J. Stone, David White, Linda Watkins, Norman Fell, John Duke.

Ness observes the attempt of a smart, beautiful girl to gain personal power by playing off underworld elements who seek her favour against each other.

30. 'Jack "Legs" Diamond' (20/10/60)

sc Charles O'Neal, story by Harry Essex *d* John Peyser
CAST: Steven Hill (as Legs Diamond), Suzanne Storrs, Lawrence Dobkin (Dutch Schultz), Robert Carricart (Lucky Luciano), Norma Crane (Alice Diamond), Ted Berger.

Based in part on the life of 'Legs' Diamond, the action centres on an incident involving the importation of a million dollars in dope, and its subsequent highjacking by Diamond (*aka* 'Clay Pigeon: The Jack "Legs" Diamond Story').

31. 'Nicky' (3/11/60)

sc Joseph Petracca *d* Walter Grauman
CAST: Luther Adler, Michael Ansara, Philip Pine, Mario Raccuzzo, Ronnie Haran, Malcolm Atterbury, Renata Vanni.

When a mobster is killed during a raid on an illicit still, Ness finds he has made a new enemy, the slain man's young son.

32. 'The Waxey Gordon Story' (10/11/60)

sc Joseph Petracca *d* John Peyser
CAST: Nehemiah Persoff (as Waxey Gordon), Frank De Kova, Sam Gilman, Lisabeth Hush, Adam Becker, Terry Huntingdon.

Ness tangles with a particularly slippery gangster when he goes after the top bootlegger of the 1930s.

33. 'The Mark of Cain' (17/11/60)

sc David Z. Goodman *d* Walter Grauman
CAST: Henry Silva, Will Kuluva.

Charlie Sabestino (Silva) is the leader of the Chicago narcotics empire, but remains outside of Ness's reach.

34. 'A Seat on the Fence' (24/11/60)

sc William P. Templeton *d* Walter Grauman
CAST: John McIntire, Arlene Sax, Frank Silvera, Olan Soule, Val Avery, Dan Barton.

Ness is thwarted when he attempts to get evidence against a ring involved in stealing narcotics from hospitals and drug stores.

35. 'The Purple Gang' (1/12/60)

sc John Mantley *d* Walter Grauman
CAST: Steve Cochran, Werner Klemperer, Steven Geray, Ilka Windish, Carl Milletaire.

Ness becomes involved with kidnapping as it was carried on in the pre-Lindbergh Law days of 1932.

36. 'Kiss of Death Girl' (8/12/60)

sc Harry Kronman *d* John Peyser
CAST: Jan Sterling, Robert H. Harris, Mickey Shaughnessy, David J. Stewart, John Conte.

Ness takes direct action when a girl whose boyfriends meet untimely deaths becomes involved in a hijacking case he has been working on.

37. 'The Larry Fay Story' (15/12/60)

sc Harry Essex *d* Walter Grauman
CAST: June Havoc, Sam Levene, Robert Emhardt, Tommy Cook, Robert Karnes, Larry Gates.

Ness investigates when racketeers force up the price of milk by strong-arm methods, and finds the trail leads to a well-known speakeasy and nightclub owner.

38. 'The Otto Frick Story' (22/12/60)

sc Leonard Kantor *d* John Peyser
CAST: Jack Warden, Francis Lederer, Richard Jaeckel, Erika Peters, John Wengraf.

Ness runs into State Department resistance after he learns that the Nazi Bund has made an alliance with dope pedlars.

39. 'The Tommy Karpeles Story' (29/12/60)

sc George Bellak *d* Stuart Rosenberg
CAST: Harold J. Stone, Madelyn Rhue, Joseph Wiseman, Murray Hamilton, Vic Morrow, Joseph Julian, Vladimir Sokoloff.

Ness dissents when a jury convicts known criminal Tommy Karpeles (Stone), on circumstantial evidence, of committing a mail robbery, and his disbelief leads to recovery of the loot.

40 and 41. 'The Big Train' [parts one! and two] (5 and 12/1/61)

sc William Spier *d* John Peyser
CAST: Neville Brand (as Al Capone), James Westerfield, Russ Conway, Louise Lorimer, Paul Bruce, Jay Hector, Russell Thorson, Richard Carlyle, Lalo Rios, Lewis McLeod, William Schallert, Eddie Firestone.

Capone's Chicago gang seal off an entire California town to spring 'Scarface' from the special train moving federal prisoners cross-country to the new federal penitentiary of Alcatraz in 1934. (Re-edited for feature release as *Alcatraz Express*.)

42. 'The Masterpiece' (19/1/61)

sc David Z. Goodman *d* Walter Grauman
CAST: Rip Torn, Robert Middleton, George Voskovec, Joseph Ruskin, Harry Shannon, Addison Richards.

Trigger expert Pittsburgh Phil (Torn), hired by Capone lieutenant Meyer Wartel (Middleton) to rub out a man who has outlived his usefulness to the mob, decides to execute the crime under the nose of Eliot Ness.

43. 'The Organization' (26/1/61)

sc Harry Kronman *d* Walter Grauman
CAST: Richard Conte, Susan Oliver, Milton Selzer, Oscar Beregi, Richard Karlan, Thom Carney.

Ness discovers a plan to organise crime throughout the country that involves taking over and expanding the Al Capone interests.

44. 'The Jamaica Ginger Story' (2/2/61)

sc Joseph Petracca *d* John Peyser
CAST: Brian Keith, Michael Ansara, James Coburn, Alfred Ryder, June Dayton.

Ness is assigned to stop the flow of Jamaica Ginger, a deadly drink from the Indies, being smuggled into America.

45. 'Augie "The Banker" Ciamino' (9/2/61)

sc Adrian Spies *d* Stuart Rosenberg
CAST: Will Kuluva, Lee Phillips, Sam Jaffe, Keenan Wynn (as Ciamino), Dean Stanton, Rebecca Welles, Bernard Kates.

Ness discovers that Ciamino, to escape detection, is having his bootleg liquor made in hundreds of home stills by honest but frightened immigrants; however, every time Ness gets a lead on a possible witness, Ciamino prevents them from testifying.

46. 'The Underground Court' (16/2/61)

sc Leonard Kantor d Don Medford
CAST: Joan Blondell, Richard Devon, Frank De Kova, John Duke, Arthur Kendall, Eddie Firestone.

Ness hunts a syndicate gangster who has disappeared with a million dollars belonging to the mob.

47. 'The Nick Moses Story' (23/2/61)

sc Tim Darlo and John Mantley, story by T. L. P. Swicegood d Herman Hoffman
CAST: Harry Guardino, Joe DeSantis, Dan Seymour, Michael Constantine, Herman Rudie, Nicki Marcelli.

A gangster defies the code of the underworld and believes he has won immunity from any reprisals by promising to eliminate Eliot Ness.

48. 'The Antidote' (9/3/61)

sc David Z. Goodman d Walter Grauman
CAST: Joseph Wiseman, Telly Savalas, Jeff Corey, Gail Robbins.

Ness acts quickly when a bootlegging ring begins using a new process to reclaim industrial alcohol that has been denatured.

49. 'The Lily Dallas Story' (16/3/61)

sc Leonard Kantor d Don Medford
CAST: Norma Crane, Larry Parks, June Vincent, Judy Strange, Linda Watkins.

When a gangland couple cannot agree on arrangements to protect their nine-year-old daughter, Ness takes advantage of the situation to solve the kidnapping of a millionaire.

50. 'Murder Under Glass' (23/3/61)

sc Harry Kronman d Walter Grauman
CAST: Luther Adler, Dennis Patrick, Carl Milletaire, Paul Birch.

Ness unmasks a New Orleans importer who is using a family firm established for six generations to bring narcotics into the country for a Chicago mob (aka 'Man Under Glass').

51. 'Testimony of Evil' (30/3/61)

sc Joseph Petracca d Paul Wendkos
CAST: David Brian, Fay Spain, John Marley, Jack Elam, Tom Fadden, Paul Genge.

Ness tries to track down a witness, hiding from the law and the mob, whose testimony can convict a gangster and influence an election.

52. 'Ring of Terror' (13/4/61)

sc John Mantley d Walter Grauman
CAST: Harold J. Stone, Viveca Lindfors, John Crawford, Sheldon Allman, Howard Caine, George Carver, Walter Burke.

Ness is thwarted in his efforts to tie in narcotics and the fight game when a victimised fight manager refuses to co-operate.

53. 'Mr Moon' (20/4/61)

sc Charles O'Neal and John Mantley d Paul Wendkos
CAST: Victor Buono, Karl Swenson, Robert Osterloh, Olan Soule.

Ness matches wits with a skilful counterfeiter who has obtained enough government paper to print $100 million worth of phoney dollars (aka 'The Counterfeit Story').

54. 'Death for Sale' (27/4/61)

sc David Z. Goodman d Stuart Rosenberg
CAST: James MacArthur, Lou Polan, Ned Glass, Carol Eastman.

A nineteen-year-old hoodlum devises a

method for selling a fortune in narcotics, then gains possession of the merchandise by strong-arm methods.

55. 'Stranglehold' (4/5/61)

sc Harry Kronman d Paul Wendkos
CAST: Ricardo Montalban, Philip Pine, Kevin Hagen, Trevor Bardette, Frank Puglia.

When a racketeer gains control of the Fulton Fish Market in New York, the authorities send to Chicago for Ness and his special squad.

56. 'The Nero Rankin Story' (11/5/61)

sc Leonard Kantor d Stuart Rosenberg
CAST: Will Kuluva, John Dehner, Joanna Moore, Richard Karlan, Brook Byron, Murvyn Vye, John Duke, Jean Carson, Barry Kelley.

The newest leader of the crime syndicate, Nero Rankin (Kuluva), threatens gang reprisals against the public if Ness continues his crackdown on the syndicate's establishments.

57. 'The Seventh Vote' (18/5/61)

sc Richard Collins d Stuart Rosenberg
CAST: Nehemiah Persoff (as Jake Guzik), Joseph Ruskin, Richard Reeves, George Neise, Robert Cornthwaite, Gregg Dunn.

Ness deals with a new underworld element when he foils a plot by Guzik and Nitti to smuggle a deported hoodlum back into the country.

58. 'The King of Champagne' (25/5/61)

sc David Z. Goodman d Walter Grauman
CAST: Robert Middleton, Barry Morse, Michael Constantine, George Kennedy.

Ness suspects the motives of a man who gives him a tip about a champagne cache, and in following the hunch discovers a plan to corner the bubbling wine market in time for the 1932 New Year's Eve celebrations.

59. 'The Nick Acropolis Story' (1/6/61)

sc Curtis Kenyon and John Mantley d Don Medford
CAST: Lee Marvin, Constance Ford, Johnny Seven.

Ness and his squad use a three-way mob fight as an opportunity to smash a bookmaking operation (aka 'The Nick Metropolous Story').

60. '90-Proof Dame' (8/6/61)

sc Harry Kronman d Walter Grauman
CAST: Steve Cochran, Joanna Barnes, Stephen Geray, Warren Stevens, Dean Stanton, Gilbert Green.

Ness tangles with Nate Kestor (Cochran), a Chicago mobster prominent in burlesque circles of show business who branches out into bootleg brandy.

Season Three

Exec prod Alan Armer; Exec in charge of prod Jerry Thorpe; Prod Lloyd Richards, Stuart Rosenberg, Del Reisman; Assoc prod Vincent McEveety, Del Reisman; Prod super James A. Paisley; Prod manager Marvin Stuart; Research Kellam De Forest; Asst dir Bud Grace, Ted Schilz; Casting Stalmaster-Lister Co.; Story ed Del Reisman; Ph Charles Straumer, Glen MacWilliams; Ph effects Howard A. Anderson Co.; Editorial super Bill Heath; Film ed Robert Watts, Ben H. Ray, Robert L. Swanson; Art dir Rolland M. Brooks, Howard Hollander, James G. Hulsey; Set decor Harry Gordon; Prop master Ken Westcott, Allan Levine; Cost Frank Delmar; Makeup Kiva Hoffman; Hair stylist Irene Beshon, Anna Malin, Jean Udko, Lorraine Roberson, Jane Chabra; Mus Nelson Riddle; Mus super Robert Raff; Sound Glen Glenn Sound Co.; Sound eng S. G. Haughton; Sound ed Ross Taylor, Joseph G. Sorokin; Nar Walter Winchell.

A Langford production in association with Desilu Productions Inc.

61. 'The Troubleshooter' (12/10/61)

sc Louis Peletier d Stuart Rosenberg
CAST: Peter Falk, Murray Hamilton, Ned Glass, Vincent Gardenia, Michael Dana, Vladimir Sokoloff.

The Chicago underworld imports a specialist in 'police contacts' from New York in an effort to keep Ness from smashing the profitable punchboard game.

62. 'Power Play' (19/10/61)

sc Harry Kronman d Paul Wendkos
CAST: Wendell Corey, Albert Salmi, Carroll O'Connor, Mary Ficket, Paul Genge.

When Ness offers full co-operation to Willard Thornton (Corey), new head of a crime commission, he is unaware that Thornton also heads an underworld syndicate.

63. 'Tunnel of Horrors' (26/10/61)

sc John Mantley d Stuart Rosenberg
CAST: Martin Balsam, Don Gordon, Joseph Ruskin.

Ness finds himself working against Max Justin (Balsam), a former police officer turned crooked, and resents the restrictions placed on honest lawmen.

64. 'The Genna Brothers' (2/11/61)

sc Harry Kronman d Paul Wendkos
CAST: Marc Lawrence (as Mike Genna), Antony Carbone (Angelo Genna), Frank Puglia, Arlene Sax, Grant Richards, Eugene Iglesias.

Ness is faced with a new problem when Chicago mobsters organise a home-still operation to keep their speakeasies supplied with liquor.

65. 'The Matt Bass Scheme' (9/11/61)

sc David Z. Goodman d Stuart Rosenberg
CAST: Telly Savalas, Grant Richards, Jaynes Barron, Herman Rudin.

The cutting off of Chicago's flow of alcohol forces the mobsters to resort to greater inventive effort, as an ex-con named Matt Bass (Savalas) devises a 'foolproof' method for bringing bootleg alcohol to Nitti.

66. 'Loophole' (16/11/61)

sc Harry Kronman d Paul Wendkos
CAST: Jack Klugman, Vaughn Taylor, Peter Brocco, Martin Landau, Gavin MacLeod, Alexander Lockwood, George Tobias.

Ness learns there is intense underworld competition for the services of a lawyer who is an expert in finding ways to evade justice.

67. 'Jigsaw' (23/11/61)

sc George Eckstein d Paul Wendkos
CAST: James Gregory, Cloris Leachman, Alan Baxter, Joe Perry, Bernie Fein.

Ness learns that the underworld has formed its own 'Untouchables' group, a counter-espionage corps that ferrets out witnesses likely to turn state's evidence.

68. 'Man Killer' (7/12/61)

sc Sy Salkowitz d Stuart Rosenberg
CAST: Ruth Roman, Ann Helm, Grant Richards, Mario Alcalde, Mario Gallo.

Ness meets Georgie (Roman), a woman shrewd enough to work her way into a partnership in the Nitti mob.

69. 'City Without a Name' (14/12/61)

sc John Mantley d Paul Wendkos
CAST: Paul Richards, Theodore Marcuse, George Keyman.

Ness finds himself in the middle of a three-way power play when he journeys east to solve the slaying of a fellow federal officer.

70. 'Hammerlock' (21/12/61)

sc Mel Goldberg *d* Stuart Rosenberg
CAST: Harold J. Stone, John Larch, Will Kuluva, Joan Staley, Robert Carricart (as Lepke).

Ness learns that a respected member of a baking industry is acting as the front man for racketeers out to get a chunk of bakery profits (*aka* 'The Bull Hanlon Story').

71. 'Canada Run' (4/1/62)

sc Barry Trivers and Harry Kronman *d* Bernard McEveety Jr
CAST: Arthur Hill, Simon Oakland, Dabbs Greer, John Alderson, Than Wyenn.

When Canadian liquor starts pouring into Chicago, Ness heads for the northern border to investigate (*aka* 'The Father Corelli Story').

72. 'Fall Guy' (11/1/62)

sc David P. Harmon *d* Bernard Kowalski
CAST: Herschel Bernardi, Jay C. Flippen, Don Gordon, Robert Emhardt, Herbie Faye.

Three hoodlums pool their special talents in a racketeering service designed to meet the problems posed by Eliot Ness and his squad.

73. 'The Gang War' (18/1/62)

sc John Mantley *d* Paul Wendkos
CAST: Victor Buono, John Kellogg, Ed Nelson, Ann Whitfield.

The shooting starts when Nitti's competitor circulates imported Scotch whisky on the bootleg market to take customers away from Nitti's speakeasies.

74. 'The Silent Partner' (1/2/62)

sc Harry Kronman *d* Abner Biberman
CAST: Charles McGraw, Allyn Joslyn, Dyan Cannon, Bert Convy.

Ness learns the hard way that even the top brass of Chicago underworld have a boss.

75. 'The Whitey Steele Story' (8/2/62)

sc George Eckstein *d* Abner Biberman
CAST: Henry Silva, Murray Hamilton, Eduardo Cianelli, Philip Pine, Sean McClory.

Ness goes underground to get evidence against the operators of a horse-racing wire service who are also peddling narcotics.

76. 'The Death Tree' (15/2/62)

sc Harry Kronman *d* Vincent McEveety
CAST: Charles Bronson, Barbara Luna, Edward Asner, Theodore Marcuse, Richard Bakalyan.

In an effort to establish a market for cheap whisky, the Capone interests appoint a renegade gypsy, Kolescu (Bronson), to head the operation.

77. 'Takeover' (1/3/62)

sc Sy Salkowitz, story by Theodore Apstein and Salkowitz *d* Bernard Kowalski
CAST: Luther Adler, Robert Loggia, Mort Mills, Leonard Nimoy, Collin Willcox, Oscar Beregi.

Ness finds Zenko (Adler) and his son Leo (Loggia) nearing a showdown over the Chicago beer market on the eve of the repeal of the Eighteenth Amendment.

78. 'The Stryker Brothers' (8/3/62)

sc Gilbert Ralston d Stuart Rosenberg
CAST: Nehemiah Persoff, Michael Strong, Frank Sutton, Joseph Bernard, Grant Richards, Buck Kartalian, Arny Freeman.

An arsonist is hired to set fire to the building which contains evidence that the three Stryker brothers committed a mail robbery to finance their illicit liquor operation.

79. 'Element of Danger' (22/3/62)

sc John Mantley d Bernard Kowalski
CAST: Lee Marvin, Victor Jory, Al Ruscio.

Victor Rate (Marvin) and Arnold Stegler (Jory) are partners who control a formula for converting opium to heroin.

80. 'The Maggie Storm Story' (29/3/62)

sc George Eckstein d Stuart Rosenberg
CAST: Patricia Neal, Vic Morrow, John Kellogg, Joseph Ruskin (as Lepke), Bernie Fein, John Harmon, Herman Rudin, Frank De Kova.

Maggie Storm (Neal) owns a swanky speakeasy which doubles as an auction room for illicit merchandise; Ness starts an investigation when a quantity of dope goes under the hammer.

81. 'Man in the Middle' (5/4/62)

sc Harry Kronman d Bernard Kowalski
CAST: Martin Balsam, Tom Drake, Cloris Leachman, Mike Mazurki, Gavin MacLeod, Joey Barnum.

Benjy Leemer (Balsam), a slot-machine operator, gives Ness information to gain personal revenge.

82. 'Downfall' (3/5/62)

sc Robert Yale Libott d Stuart Rosenberg

CAST: Steven Hill, Simon Oakland, Milton Selzer, Stefan Schnabel.

Ness does not suspect that the scion of a respectable railroad family is allied with racketeers until bootleg whisky starts pouring into Chicago from Canada via a well-known line.

83. 'The Case Against Eliot Ness' (10/5/62)

sc George Eckstein d Bernard Kowalski
CAST: Pat Hingle, Jeanne Cooper, Cliff Carnell, Joseph Turkel.

An ambitious public figure, Mitchell Grandin (Hingle), tries to take over the 1933 Chicago World's Fair.

84. 'The Ginnie Littlesmith Story' (17/5/62)

sc Leonard Kantor d Stuart Rosenberg
CAST: Phyllis Love, Don Gordon, Brook Byron, Linda Evans, Jeno Mate, Leonard Strong, Marlene Callahan.

Ginnie Littlesmith (Love) claims the records of a deceased hoodlum as an inheritance from her uncle, but Ness needs the books so he can prosecute the racketeers who have set a price on the volumes.

85. 'The Contract' (31/5/62)

sc George Eckstein d Bernard Kowalski

CAST: Harry Guardino, Frank Sutton, Gloria Talbott, John Larkin, Oscar Beregi.

Ness pursues a hoodlum to a gambling ship anchored off the California coast.

86. 'Pressure' (14/6/62)

sc Harry Kronman d Vincent McEveety
CAST Harold J. Stone, Darryl Hickman, Warren Oates, Collin Willcox, Booth Colman.

A top syndicate narcotics dealer warns Ness that any interference with his activities will mean the destruction of a school while classes are in session.

or federal law making the sale of machine-guns illegal.

87. 'Arsenal' (28/6/62)

sc John Mantley *d* Paul Wendkos
CAST: George Mathews, Salome Jens, Kevin Hagen, Karl Swenson.

A gang war threatens when Chicago hoods discover there is no local, state

88. 'The Monkey Wrench' (5/7/62)

sc George Eckstein *d* Bernard Kowalski
CAST: Dolores Dorn, Claude Akins, Oscar Beregi, Cliff Osmond, Albert Szabo.

A gangster's widow permits Frank Nitti to use her north-country home in an underworld smuggling operation.

Season Four

Exec prod Leonard Freeman; *Exec in charge of prod* Jerry Thorpe; *Prod* Alvin Cooperman, Alan Armer, Lloyd Richards; *Assoc prod* Del Reisman; *Prod super* James A. Paisley; *Prod manager* Marvin Stuart; *Research* Kellam De Forest; *Asst dir* Ted Schilz, Bud Grace, Russ Haverick; *Casting* Stalmaster-Lister Co.; *Ph* Charles Straumer, Glen MacWilliams; *Ph effects* Howard A. Anderson Co.; *Editorial super* Bill Heath; *Film ed* Ben H. Ray, Robert Watts, Axel Hubert, Frank O'Neill, Robert L. Swanson; *Art dir* Rolland M. Brooks, Howard Hollander, Frank T. Smith, James Hulsey; *Set decor* Harry Gordon, Frank Tuttle; *Prop master* Allan Levine, Don D. Smith; *Cost* Frank Delmar, Seth Banks; *Makeup* Kiva Hoffman, Dick Smith, Louis J. Haszillo, Adelbert Acevido, David Newell; *Hair stylist* Jean Udko, Joan St Oegger, Jane Chabra, Jackie Bone, Hazel Keithley, Merle Reeves, Armienne Forgette; *Mus* Nelson Riddle, Leith Stevens, Alexander Courage, Pete Rugolo; *Mus super* Wilbur Hatch; *Mus co-ord* Julian Davidson; *Mus ed* Robert Raff; *Sound* Glen Glenn Sound Co.; *Sound eng* S. G. Haughton, James S. Thomson; *Sound ed* Ross Taylor, Joseph G. Sorokin; *Nar* Walter Winchell.

A Langford production in association with Desilu Productions.

89. 'The Night They Shot Santa Claus' (25/9/62)

sc Mort Thaw *d* Alex March
CAST: Ruth White, Nita Talbot, Murvyn Vye, Russell Collins, Isabel Jewell, Grace Lee Whitney, John Duke.

Ness unravels the threads of the dual life led by a man killed by gangsters; supposedly happily married and involved in charity work, he was, however, bound to the underworld.

90. 'Cooker in the Sky' (2/10/62)

sc John D. F. Black *d* Robert Butler
CAST: Milton Selzer, J. D. Cannon, Anne Jackson.

Chicago mobsters import a brewery expert from New York to construct a 'Ness-proof' plant.

91. 'The Chess Game' (9/10/62)

sc David Z. Goodman *d* Stuart Rosenberg
CAST: Richard Conte, Murray Hamilton, Michael Constantine, Barbara Barrie, Ned Glass.

Ness tangles with a blind Boston fish merchant who finds the refrigerated freight cars of his trade ideal for transporting champagne.

92. 'The Economist' (16/10/62)

sc Harold Gast *d* Paul Stanley

CAST: Joseph Sirola, Ellen Madison, George Mathews.

An educated mobster plans to dry up Chicago's whisky supply until Depression prices rise.

93. 'The Pea' (23/10/62)

sc Harry Kronman d Paul Stanley
CAST: Frank Gorshin, Sally Gracie, Albert Paulsen, Gilbert Greene, Elizabeth MacRae, Stefan Gierasch.

When a young pool player's activities plunge him into debt, Ness lends him money in exchange for information.

94. 'Bird in the Hand' (30/10/62)

sc Harry Kronman d Walter Grauman
CAST: Dane Clark, Herschel Bernardi, Carroll O'Connor, Nan Martin, Joseph Schildkraut, John Gabriel.

Ness tracks a small time hoodlum from Chicago to Washington, DC, and finds that the Health Department is also interested in the case.

95. 'The Eddie O'Gara Story' (13/11/62)

sc Carey Wilbur d Robert Butler
CAST: Michael Connors, Robert J. Wilke (as Bugs Moran), Sean McClory, Meg Wyllie.

Mobster Eddie O'Gara (Connors) returns to Chicago after three years and offers to help his ex-boss Bugs Moran regain his position of power.

96. 'Elegy' (20/11/62)

sc Herman Groves and Harold Gast d Robert Butler
CAST: Barbara Stanwyck, John Larch, Peggy Ann Garner, Bill Sargent.

A dying gangster asks for Ness's help in locating his missing daughter; Ness calls on Aggie Stewart (Stanwyck) of the Missing Persons' Bureau for assistance.

97. 'Come and Kill Me' (27/11/62)

sc Kitty Buhler d Robert Gist
CAST: Dan Dailey, Ted De Corsia, Robert Brice.

Ness links a karate expert, who trains teenage boys as killers, with an underworld extermination expert.

98. 'A Fist of Five' (4/12/62)

sc Herman Groves d Ida Lupino
CAST: Lee Marvin, Frank De Kova, Phyllis Coates, James Caan, Roy Thinnes, Mark Allen, Whitney Armstrong.

Frustrated by his inability to make arrests stick, a dedicated policeman forms an illicit mob with his four brothers.

99. 'The Floyd Gibbons Story' (11/12/62)

sc George Eckstein d Robert Butler
CAST: Scott Brady, Stuart Erwin, Dorothy Malone, Alan Baxter, Norman Burton, Lee Krieger, Paul Langton, Jerry Oddo.

A famed war correspondent helps Ness solve the slaying of a reporter friend and uncover a diabolical underworld operation.

100. 'Doublecross' (18/12/62)

sc John Mantley d Paul Wendkos
CAST: Nehemiah Persoff (as Jake Guzik), Harry Morgan (as Bugs Moran), John Duke, John Kellogg, Mal Throne.

Ness temporarily becomes a bootlegger to halt the activities of Jake Guzik.

101. 'Search for a Dead Man' (1/1/63)

sc Herman Groves and Harold Gast d Robert Butler

CAST: Barbara Stanwyck (as Lt Agatha Stewart), Virginia Capers, Edward Asner, Alan Dexter, Carlo Tricoli.

An unidentified body marked for burial in Potter's Field receives an elaborate funeral wreath which suggests gangster connections.

102. 'The Speculator' (8/1/63)

sc Max Ehrlich d Allen Reisner
CAST: Telly Savalas, Frank Sutton, Ted Knight.

Ness takes advantage of the situation when a young financial wizard tries to fleece Frank Nitti.

103. 'The Snowball' (15/1/63)

sc Norman Katkov d Alex March
CAST: Robert Redford, Gerald Hiken, Robert Bice.

A college graduate conducts a profitable whisky trade on various campuses.

104. 'Jake Dance' (22/1/63)

sc Gilbert Ralston d Robert Butler
CAST: Dane Clark, Sondra Kerr, Joe DeSantis, Liam Sullivan, John Gabriel, Linda Watkins, Joseph Schildkraut.

Ness engineers a jail delivery to free a mobster who can lead him to the head of the ring which has been flooding Chicago with poisoned liquor.

105. 'Blues for a Gone Goose' (29/1/63)

sc Don Brinkley d Sherman Marks
CAST: Kathy Nolan, Robert Duval, Will Kuluva, Marc Lawrence, Richard Bakalyan.

The wife of a Chicago mobster falls for a jazz club trumpet player, and the resulting triangle opens the door for Ness to step in.

106. 'Globe of Death' (5/2/63)

sc John Mantley d Walter Grauman
CAST: Phil Pine, Cliff Osmond, Gilbert Green, Mal Thorne.

Ness learns that a $2 million dope shipment has reached Chicago from the Far East.

107. 'Eye for an Eye' (19/2/63)

sc John D. F. Black d Robert Butler
CAST: Jack Klugman, George Voskovec.

Ness meets a hoodlum who has developed a virtually foolproof scheme for defeating the government's programme to stop the sale of liquor.

108. 'Junk Man' (26/2/63)

sc Herman Groves d Paul Wendkos
CAST: Pat Hingle, Joe DeSantis, Edward Binns, Joan Chambers, Michael Constantine, Jerry Oddo.

Ness learns that a prime suspect in a narcotics case is actually an undercover agent of another government agency.

109. 'Man in the Cooler' (5/3/63)

sc John D. F. Black d Ida Lupino
CAST: J. D. Cannon, Peter Whitney, Salome Jens, Eddie Firestone, I. Stanford Jolley.

Ness ventures into a federal prison and releases a convicted bootlegger to get help in smashing a huge liquor ring.

110. 'The Butcher's Boy' (12/3/63)

sc Harry Kronman d Allen Reisner
CAST: Frank Sutton, John Larkin, Francine York, Barney Phillips, H. M. Wynant, Jay Novello.

A First World War Croix de Guerre and a beautiful brunette become unexpected aids when Ness goes after an extortion ring.

111. 'The Spoiler' (26/3/63)

sc Tony Barrett d Laslo Benedek
CAST: Rip Torn, Tim Considine, Claude Akins, Virginia Christine.

Both Ness and an underworld figure are in pursuit of a gangster who has secretly returned from Brazil to pick up the $200,000 in loot he left behind when he fled.

112. 'One Last Killing' (2/4/63)

sc Harold Gast d Allen Reisner
CAST: Don Gordon, Harold Stone, Jeanne Cooper, Johnny Seven, Woodrow Parfrey.

Rival hoodlums double-cross each other, then throw false clues to Ness.

113. 'The Giant Killer' (9/4/63)

sc George Eckstein d Leonard Horn
CAST: Paul Richards, Karl Lukas, Peggy Ann Garner, Torin Thatcher, Patty Regan.

A convicted racketeer suspects that his son-in-law set him up for the arrest, and orders Janos (Lukas), his muscle man, to check it out, unaware that Janos has long been in love with his employer's daughter.

114. 'The Charlie Argos Story' (16/4/63)

sc Harry Kronman, story by Robert Yale Libott d Leonard Horn
CAST: Patricia Owens, Robert Vaughn, Kent Smith, Stefan Gierasch, Chris Dark, Stanley Adams.

Ness refuses a fat fee to act as executor of the estate of a dying mobster, and to accept the responsibility of finding the man's long-lost son.

115. 'The Jazz Man' (30/4/63)

sc David Goodman d Vincent McEveety
CAST: Simon Oakland, Robert Emhardt, Jacqueline Scott, Cliff Carnell, Steven Geray, Robert Ellin, Robert Bice.

Ness, impersonating a slain musician, journeys to New Orleans to investigate the source of narcotics being shipped to Chicago.

116. 'The Torpedo' (7/5/63)

sc Ed Adamson d Ida Lupino
CAST: Charles McGraw, John Anderson, Gail Kobe, John Milford, James Griffith.

Ness fosters a situation in which an ageing gunman who has lost his nerve is no longer able to carry out his gangland boss's orders.

117. 'Line of Fire' (14/5/63)

sc Tony Barrett d Robert Butler
CAST: Ed Nelson, Joe DeSantis, Sherwood Price, Ford Rainey, Grace Lee Whitney, Richard Bakalyan.

Ness becomes involved when the mentally disturbed brother of a gangland lord starts a gang war.

118. 'A Taste for Pineapple' (21/5/63)

sc Will Lorin d Alex March
CAST: Jeremy Slate, Tom Tully, Edward Binns, Robert Yuro.

When Ness learns that underworld big shots are scrambling from Chicago to distant cities, he knows they are establishing alibis for something big; little does he suspect, however, that he is to be the victim of their scheme.

Index